To
Mary Karen
God Bless

Love A-H Mo
Lois
Manh 16-84

Sandy Ground Memories

SANDY
Memories

INCLUDING

Family Stories

by Other Sandy Grounders

THE STATEN ISLAND HISTORICAL SOCIETY

GROUND

by Lois A. H. Mosley

INTRODUCTION AND

ADDITIONAL ESSAYS BY

Barnett Shepherd

STATEN ISLAND, NEW YORK   2003

Published by The Staten Island Historical Society,

441 Clarke Avenue, Staten Island, New York 10301.

Library of Congress Catalogue Number: [to come]

Designed by Bruce McPherson and produced by Bound to Last.

Printed in the United States of America.

Contents

(5)

PART THREE

Family Stories by Other Sandy Grounders

PART FOUR

Sandy Ground Street by Street

Preface

I T IS A PRIVILEGE for the Staten Island Historical Society to publish Lois A. H. Mosley's *Sandy Ground Memories*. This publication represents a continuation of the Society's commitment to Sandy Ground's history begun by Minna Cheves Wilkins in the 1940s. Miss Wilkins wrote the pioneering article, "Sandy Ground: A Tiny Racial Island," which was published in 1943 in the *Staten Island Historian*, the Society's journal.

Miss Wilkins, upon her retirement as a profesisonal psychologist, became a volunteer in the Society's library specializing in genealogical research. It was there she took up her research on Sandy Ground. Her article was based on an exhaustive amount of library research and extensive interviews with Sandy Ground residents. With this she produced the first factual account of the community and its inhabitants. This pioneering work is often overlooked today, but without it a whole generation of living history would have been lost. Miss Wilkins's article was reprinted in the Summer 1989 issue of the *Staten Island Historian*. Editor John B. Woodall provided an introduction with much information about her.

In more recent years, under the leadership of Executive Director Barnett Shepherd, the *Historian* published Ronald David Jackson's article, "The Freedom Seekers: Staten Island's Runaway Slaves" (Summer 1996). Mr. Jackson compiled an unpublished listing of Staten Island slaveholders and slaves. His work was accomplished with a grant to the Staten Island Historical Society from the New York State Council on the Arts. Another NYSCA grant enabled the Society to employ Annette Marks-Ellis to research and draft an African American history of Staten Island. It is being integrated into Historic Richmond Town's educational programs, including the curriculum offered to the 15,000 schoolchildren who visit Historic Richmond Town each year.

Sandy Ground Memories gives us new understanding and appreciation of the important role African Americans have played in Staten Island's history. I hope that you will enjoy reading it and that you will join us in learning more about all aspects of our community's history.

Special thanks to those members of the Staten Island Historical Society who have generously contributed to its John Frederick Smith Publication Fund to enable this book to be printed. They include: Mr. Irving R. Boody Jr., Mr. James R. Coyle, Miss Helen M. Cusack, Mr. Bruce Gillam, Dr. and Mrs. Albert L. Patrick, Mr. and Mrs. Peter J. Salvatore, and Mrs. John B. Woodall.

JOHN W. GUILD
Executive Director
The Staten Island Historical Society

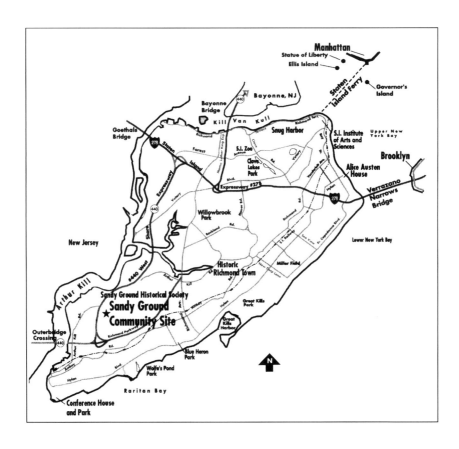

Foreword

L OIS MOSLEY has done what most of us say we want to do, but never get around to: Write down memories of family and friends. The story of her life is remarkable. I appreciate her openness, frankness, and willingness to tell a white man like me all about Sandy Ground. Mrs. Mosley's interest in history has opened many doors to my own research and understanding. It is a privilege to read her manuscript and learn her family story. She has expanded our knowledge of Sandy Ground's history.

The Sandy Ground community emerged in 1850 with the founding of the Rossville A.M.E. Zion Church. It may not be the oldest African American community in the New York metropolitan region, but it has had a long and continuous existence, shaping and molding the lives of the people who lived there, and their descendants, in many powerful ways. It is a vital and beloved part of American history.

Mrs. Mosley's first Sandy Ground ancestor settled there before 1850. Since then four generations have lived in this community. For many years she has collected and preserved valuable memorabilia, including beautiful historic photographs. I have helped to organize these materials and clarify her genealogical history. Her family generation chart is provided in the appendix. Succeeding generations of her family as well as future historians will be able to gain a more complete understanding of Sandy Ground.

The Great Depression of the 1930s shaped the background of Lois Mosley's childhood in Sandy Ground, as it did to many children in urban and rural areas across the country. Sandy Ground was then a community of African American families and individuals eking out a dignified life with meager resources. Many were courageous families cherishing a sense of history and supportive of one another in their bonds of race and community. Having survived the end of the Staten Island oyster industry in which their grandfathers and great-grandfathers had flourished, they shared common bonds as a community. Parents remembered better times, told their children about them, and found new fields of endeavor.

Mrs. Mosley's pursuit of higher education and a professional career, against all odds of poverty and the prejudices of some white Staten Islanders, is an inspiration. She remains balanced and hopeful.

Sandy Ground was primarily a close-knit community of African Americans, many of whom intermarried. Mr. George Hunter said of the Crabtree Avenue cemetery, "Those graves over there all grown up in cockleburs are Jackson graves, Jacksons and Henrys and Landins. Most of the people lying in here were related to each other, some by blood, some by marriage, some close, some distant. If you started in at the gate and ran an imaginary line all the way through, showing who was related to who, the line would zigzag all over the cemetery." ("Mr. Hunter's Grave," by Joseph Mitchell, 1956.)

Sandy Ground residents often used the terms "aunt," "uncle" or "cousin" as honorific titles of nearly every admired older citizen.

A number of white families also lived in Sandy Ground, such as those residing on the south side of Sharrott's Road, who lived in peaceful proximity to African American families. A few lived "next door," along Bloomingdale and Woodrow Roads. Lois recalls: "At the very beginning of Clay Pit Road lived a few white families: The Wogloms, O'Sheas, McKinleys, Reillys and a few others. During my childhood color had no meaning to the people in Sandy Ground. We did not experience prejudice in Sandy Ground; we got along with our neighbors white or black. Mrs. Evangeline O'Shea and Mrs. Schleigner on Sharrott's Road were best friends of my mother."

Sandy Ground is remembered today primarily as an historic community of African American oystermen. From the second half of the 19th century into the early 20th, the products of their labor and skill delighted the palates of prosperous New Yorkers and residents of other American cities. The community they created established deep and long-lasting roots. It is a unique part of New York City's history. I hope this illustrated volume will make its history known to a wider audience and offer some atonement for the loss of nearly all of Sandy Ground's physical traces.

— BARNETT SHEPHERD

PART ONE

Beginnings

How Sandy Ground Began and Flourished

Barnett Shepherd

IN 1850, 76 years before Lois Mosley's birth, Sandy Ground was established in Westfield, the most rural township of Richmond County, Staten Island, New York. One of Staten Island's four original townships, which had been officially designated in 1788, Westfield was populated by old Staten Island families of Dutch and Huguenot descent with names like Winant, Guyon and Woglom. They were farmers, businessmen and oystermen. The predominant religion in Westfield was Methodist.[1]

The Arthur Kill formed Westfield's coastline on the north and west, with the Raritan Bay on the south. The northern coast included Rossville Bay and the southern coast Prince's Bay. (See map of Westfield, page 35) Westfield's extensive coastline and natural harbors made it accessible to New York City by boat. Daily steam ferry service to and from Manhattan and New Jersey, starting in the latter half of the 19th century, made Rossville Westfield's transportation center.

Since its earliest settlement Staten Island had been widely known for the high quality of its oysters, and particularly those obtained from the waters of Prince's Bay, four miles from the future site of Sandy Ground. But by the beginning of the 19th century, with the growing demand from the metropolitan region's rapidly increasing population, Staten Island's natural oyster beds were nearly depleted. Oystermen working at Prince's Bay then obtained seed oysters from other Staten Island waterways and planted them in Prince's Bay. They soon began transplanting seed from Long Island. By 1816 oysters arrived from the Chesapeake Bay for sale in New York City markets and by 1820 seed oysters from the Chesapeake were being planted in Prince's Bay.[2] The oyster seed were placed on the bay floor in the spring, matured during the summer, and were harvested in the fall. The seeding and harvesting of oysters were physically demanding jobs available to both white and African American laborers.

Oystering was not Westfield's sole economic base. Jobs as laborers on Westfield's farms were also plentiful. The flat or gently rolling land held many fertile farms. The *Richmond County Register,* an 1862 directory in the collection of the Staten Island Historical Society, states that its soil was "a sandy loam mixed with clay." It notes, "...certain parts of Westfield are unusually productive farms." In 1910 a Staten Island newspaper reported, "Sandy Ground is the most fertile garden spot of Greater New York. The Agricultural Society invited people down there who grow things to exhibit them at the county Fair." (*Staten Island World,* Sept. 3, 1910, cited by Hugh Powell.)

THE NAME "SANDY GROUND"

When did the name "Sandy Ground" come into use? The earliest written reference to it is in 1854 in the records of St. Luke's Episcopal Church at Rossville. The list of communicants includes Silas and Ann Harris and gives their place of residence: "Silas Harris (colored) in woods near Sandy Ground road."[3]

The 1797 map of Staten Island shows "Sandy Brook" beginning north of today's Woodrow Road and flowing southward into today's Lemon Creek.[4] The name of this stream, together with the "sandy loam" makeup of the soil, appears to have determined the region's name.

When the A.M.E. Zion church was founded, the name "Rossville" may have been chosen because it was the closest town and the post office was located there. By the early decades of the 20th century, Sandy

Grounders often gave their address as "Pleasant Plains," where their post office had by then relocated and where they shopped. The post office was opposite the train station.

Located on high ground between Rossville and Prince's Bay, the area that became the African American community of Sandy Ground was wooded, as described in deeds.[5] Because the site was not on the waterfront, nor near the railroad proposed in 1850 and running by 1860, nor cleared for farming, land there was available at lower cost.

THE BEGINNING AND GROWTH OF SANDY GROUND

African Americans, both slave and free, have lived on Staten Island since the earliest European settlement. David Pietersz de Vries, the leader of Staten Island's first colony, refers in a journal entry of Feb. 10, 1640, to a "negro" who watched "...my swine and those of the Company."[6] Census records of the late 18th and early 19th centuries show that African Americans, slave or free, usually lived singly, as servants and laborers, within the households of white families.

During the 1840s, and continuing into the century, hundreds of thousands of impoverished Irish and German people arrived in the port of New York. Thousands of them settled in New York City.[7] Staten Island also changed dramatically with the influx of these new groups. Especially on the eastern shore, in Stapleton and its environs, many German and Irish immigrants made their homes.

At this time African Americans also began to move from Manhattan to Staten Island. Census records and deed books indicate that the majority of Sandy Ground's settlers in the 1850s and 1860s were born in New York City and New York State. They settled in remote Westfield, in part to escape the crowded ghettos of the city rapidly being occupied by Irish and German immigrants.

THE ROSSVILLE A.M.E. ZION CHURCH

The date of Dec. 9, 1850, stands out as the beginning of Sandy Ground's formal history. In a congregational meeting on that day the election of trustees of the Rossville A.M.E. Zion Church took place. This election would strongly suggest the prior existence of church services and other church activities. The Rossville A.M.E. Zion Church and its first minister, William H. Pitts, should probably be credited with the emergence of Sandy Ground as a viable African American community.[8]

Fifteen months later, on April 17, 1852, two of the new church's named trustees, John Henry and Francis Williams, registered the results of the election at "the African Zion Methodist Episcopal Church in the village of Rossville" at the Richmond County Clerk's and Surrogate's Office.

"In our place of meeting on the 9th of December, 1850," they stated, "the following persons were duly elected by a plurality of voices to serve as Trustees of the church: Caesar Jackson, Francis Williams, John Henry, Hiram Jones and William Henry Stephens."

This record (recorded in Liber 25, Page 513) in the Richmond County Clerk's register of deeds is the earliest written document to record both the beginning of the church and the existence of the Sandy Ground community. It would appear that the trustees were considering purchasing land in preparation for construction of a church building. In any case, their action made the existence of the church a legal fact.

THE CHURCH TRUSTEES

Each of these church trustees is listed in the 1850 Census for Westfield. Each has the letter "B" signifying their race, following the listing of their age. Caesar Jackson, 48, "laborer," born New York; Francis Williams, 45, "laborer," born New York; John Henry, 30, "a boatman", born New York; Hiram Jones, 28, "mariner" (no birthplace given); and William Henry Stephens, 42, (no vocation given), born Delaware. Hiram Jones is listed as having assets of $1,000. He is the only one of the five whose assets are listed.

Some additional information is known about four of these leaders:

CAESAR JACKSON was the son of John Jackson, captain of the ferryboat *Lewis Columbia*, that travelled between Rossville and New York.[9] John Jackson made three purchases of land in Westfield between 1828 and 1838.[10] His grave marker, "Captain John Jackson," is the oldest surviving headstone in the A.M.E. Zion cemetery.[11]

JOHN HENRY is John J. (Jackson) Henry, Lois Mosley's great-grandfather (see Lois Mosley's generation chart on page 235). John J. Henry's mother, Frances Jackson Henry, was John Jackson's sister. Caesar Jackson therefore was John Henry's cousin. John J. Henry's son, Francis M. Henry, Lois Mosley's grandfather, became a prominent oysterman and leader of the Sandy Ground church and community. John J. Henry became prosperous through the oyster industry. The 1850 Census listed him as "boatman," the 1855 Census as "farmer." No listing appears in the 1860 Census, but in the 1875 Census he is called "oysterman."

By tradition, he was the owner of an oyster sloop, the *Fanny Fern*, a 30-footer.[12] According to William "Pop" Pedro, the *Fanny Fern* carried oysters to market in Manhattan.[13] ("Fanny Fern" was the pen name of Sara Payson Willis Parton [1811-1872], a popular writer. One of her books, *Fern Leaves from Fanny's Port-Folio*, sold 70,000 copies in 1853.[14] She became a regular contributor to the *New York Ledger*, a literary magazine.[15])

WILLIAM HENRY STEPHENS is listed in the 1855 Census with letter "M" for mulatto following his name. A farmer, he had resided in Westfield for seven years, having arrived ca. 1848, and was born in Maryland. The value of his house was $100.

FRANCIS WILLIAMS is in the 1860 Census listed as "farm laborer," his house valued at $1,000 and other assets at $300. His birthplace is given as New Jersey (differing from the New York birthplace given in the 1850 Census). His wife, Grace, aged 44, was born in New Jersey.

HIRAM JONES does not appear in any Staten Island census after 1850. He may have moved away or died.

A second early document vital to understanding the history of the church and the Sandy Ground community is also on file in the County Clerk's Office (Liber 33, Page 155). It records a sale of land to the newly established church. The sale was made on Dec. 11, 1852, and recorded on Feb. 18, 1854. The "African Methodist Church" bought, for $75, three quarters of an acre from James S. Guyon and his wife Priscilla. Four of the same trustees' names appear on this document: Caesar Jackson, Francis Williams, John Henry and William H. Stephens. A fifth person, William Webb, is a new trustee, about whom no information has been discovered.

OTHER FIRST SETTLERS

In addition to these church trustees, another name emerges among the earliest settlers of the community.

According to Hubbell's history of Methodism on Staten Island (1898), the meeting of Dec. 9, 1850, took place in the home of WILLIAM H. PITTS, who on that date was appointed pastor of the church.[16] The 1850 Census states that Pitts was black, aged 40, "a Methodist clergyman," born in Virginia in 1810. His assets are listed as $600. His wife, Mary, aged 35, was born in North Carolina. The formality and specificity of his vocation are unusual in a census listing, suggesting his major standing in the community.

Most A.M.E. Zion ministers at this time were also employed in secular jobs. Indeed, the 1860 Census lists Pitts' vocation as "laborer," his assets, $800. Pitts is documented as an A.M.E. Zion clergyman in the New York Conference listing of 1860. In 1864 he was appointed to a committee representing the New York Conference at a church union convention.[17] His later career is undocumented.

OWNERSHIP OF LAND

Pitts' role was a central one in the community as well as in the church. A deed in the County Clerk's office recorded on May 21, 1849, indicates that Pitts, of New York County, purchased two acres of land from Bornt P. Winant, "on the public road running from Rossville to Richmond Valley" (this road was later named Bloomingdale Road) for $400 (Liber 18, Page 693). This is the earliest recorded land transaction of an African American clearly associated with Sandy Ground.

MOSES K. HARRIS AND HARRISVILLE

The second earliest deed by African American MOSES K. HARRIS of New York City is dated August 3, 1850 (Liber 21, Page 325). It records the purchase of a three-acre plot adjoining Pitts' land to the west. Located off the main road it sold for $287.50, a lesser price than Pitts paid. The sellers were James S. Guyon and his wife Priscilla Ann. The plot was located west of today's Bloomingdale Road, not far from its intersection with Woodrow Road.

Eleven months later Moses sold one acre of this land to SILAS K. HARRIS, his brother.

Moses K. Harris is listed for the first time in the 1855 Census. His racial category is "M" for mulatto. He is listed as "laborer," aged 35, having resided in Westfield three years (arrived ca. 1852). His place of birth is illegible, but Orange, N.J. is given in later censuses. Interviews with descendants give his mother's family name as Keys (hence the "K.") and state that she was a Mohawk Indian.[18]

The deed books between 1854 and 1897 show five other Westfield land purchases by Moses K. Harris. In 1854 he bought land in Stapleton for $600. The 1875 Census states that he was a fruit grower born in New Jersey. His wife Louisa J. was black and born in Virginia. Hubbell's church history mentions Moses K. Harris as a Deacon in the Rossville A.M.E. Zion Church and specifies that he was appointed in 1875 to meet with the bishop concerning a controversy.[19] An 1890-1891 directory lists his vocation as "vendor" and his residence as Stapleton.[20]

"Harrisville" as the "official" name for Sandy Ground was published by William T. Davis in 1896.[21] Although Moses K. Harris and Silas K. Harris as Sandy Ground pioneers are nearly forgotten today, they deserve to be remembered as central figures to the establishment of the community.

Knowledge of Silas K. Harris was handed down to us by his son Isaac, who lived until 1956 and whose oral history interviews survive. Silas and his wife Ann were Episcopalians who attended St. Luke's Church, a predominately white congregation, in Rossville. They are buried in the Silver Mount Cemetery, located on Victory Boulevard opposite Silver Lake. In 1872, when Silas purchased Plot 180, this was a whites-only cemetery and their burial there was highly unusual.[22] (More about Isaac Harris in the caption for his residence, 444 Bloomingdale Road.)

MARYLAND'S FREE BLACKS

Maryland, a slave state, had an unusually large number of free African American residents, especially in the Chesapeake area. They were believed to threaten the institution of slavery and the state legislature sought ways to limit their freedom and growth. In the 1850s harsh state laws were enacted that penalized black oystermen. They were not allowed to own sloops or captain a sloop without a white man present.

The legislature paid free blacks' transportation to Liberia and even offered a stipend to those relocating there.[23]

Walling's map (1859) records three names of African Americans not yet mentioned: M. Purnell, E. Bishop and J. Bishop. These are surnames of Maryland origin, as confirmed in census records. According to tradition, Maryland Sandy Grounders come from Snow Hill, Worcester County, on Maryland's Eastern Shore.

M. Purnell probably refers to Minnie Purnell (his first name is variously spelled). He is listed in the 1855 Westfield Census as aged 50, farmer, born Maryland. His wife Sophia, aged 50, was born in Virginia. The earliest purchase of property by Minnie (or Menil) Purnell is recorded in the Staten Island deed books (Liber 67, Page 296) in 1866, when other Purnells also purchased Staten Island property. The 1859 map may be interpreted as meaning that M. Purnell was occupying one of the Moses K. Harris properties, not necessarily that he owned the land.

I can find nothing more about the E. Bishop whose name appears on the 1859 map. Joseph Bishop is listed in the 1855 Census, aged 40, "B" for black, a laborer. In the 1860 Census "M" for mulatto follows his name. His assets were $750. According to his grandson, he was a woodworker who was born in Snow Hill, Maryland, and died in 1900. His son William A. Bishop (d. 1934) established a blacksmith business on Woodrow Road in 1888. The business was continued into the 20th century by his son Joseph (1906-1986).[24]

THE LANDINS AND THE GOLDEN AGE OF SANDY GROUND

In the 1860s and 1870s other African Americans came to settle in Sandy Ground from the Chesapeake Bay area of Maryland, Virginia and Delaware. By the 1880s a number had become prosperous oystermen.

The 1880s and 1890s were Sandy Ground's "Golden Age." Sandy

Ground had become a cohesive community of African Americans residing in perhaps 50 houses. A large percentage owned their own property.
The largest, most expensive houses were built during this period, as were
two churches, the Mount Zion A.M.E. Church (1880) and the new building for the Rossville A.M.E. Zion Church (1897).

The Landin brothers (there are variant spellings of "Landin") became the most famous of Sandy Ground's oystermen. They first appear
in the 1875 Westfield Census. Dawson Landin and Robert Landin
bought land in 1862 (Liber 50, Page 197) and 1863 (Liber 52, Page
203) on what is today's Sharrott's Road. They made several more purchases in the 1870s and 1880s.

The 1875 Census lists Dawson Landin (b. 1828) as an "oyster grower."
He was the first black Sandy Ground resident to own a sloop, the *Pacific,* a 40-footer, which was used to bring seed from the Chesapeake,
and for other long-distance work. He sold oyster seed to white oystermen.[25] Dawson Landin was Lois Mosley's maternal great-grandfather.

Robert Landin (b. 1830) is first listed as "oysterman" in the 1875
Census. He owned a 30-foot sloop, the *Independence.* After the closing
of the oyster beds in 1916 his boat lay on the beach at Prince's Bay and
rotted away.[26]

Dawson Landin Jr. (b. 1870), who followed his father into the oyster
business, was Lois Mosley's maternal grandfather. By about 1900 he
had become the richest man in Sandy Ground and often its community
spokesperson. He was well liked by all. It is said that he carried $500 in
cash and would lend it generously.[27] "Daws" sold the *Pacific* when the
oyster beds were closed.[28]

Robert H. Landin (1854-1934) was also a prosperous oysterman,
although he did not own a sloop. Born in Talbot County, Maryland, he
may have been related to the Landin brothers, but the exact relationship

has not yet been determined. Maude Landin, who contributed a chapter to this book, was a daughter of Robert H. Landin. Norma Wallen McGhie, another contributor, is a granddaughter.

The Henmans and the Purnells were other Sandy Grounders who led the oyster trade and prospered in it. There were probably others whose names have not been handed down to us.

ESTHER V. S. PURNELL (1836?-1905)

Esther V. S. Purnell is a legendary heroine of Sandy Ground's Golden Age. According to tradition, she started the first school there. Minna Wilkins, writing in 1943, says that Esther Purnell taught in Sandy Ground for more than 50 years. Although Wilkins does not document this information, she often gives her oral history source as John Henman.[29] William "Pop" Pedro and other community leaders also spoke of Esther Purnell as Sandy Ground's first teacher.[30]

Her maiden name appears in the will of William Purnell, filed on June 3, 1875. "And lastly I nominate my friends Dawson Landon Executor and my friend Esther V. Smith executrix of this my last Will and Testament...." (Liber of Wills N, Page 191.) Her name appears in the 1860 census for Worcester County (Snow Hill), Maryland, and in the Westfield census for 1870.

Yvonne Taylor of Eltingville has inherited from Rebecca Gray Landin of Sandy Ground, her maternal grandmother, a children's book titled *Dialogue Between a Brother and Sister, Concerning Salvation by Christ, and Other Books for Young Children*, published by the American Tract Society, undated. It is inscribed, "A reward of merit to Rebecca Gray from her teacher, Esther V. Smith, June 13, 1873."

The 1875 Census lists Esther Smith, aged 39, color black, occupation house keeper. No other person is listed in her household. When she married George Purnell has not been documented. Robinson's map of 1898 shows her name, E.V.S. Purnell, on a lot on an unnamed street west of Bloomingdale Road.

It is possible that Esther's school was in the A.M.E. Zion Church. This would be in keeping with the important educational roles of black churches. She may have taught religion as well as "the three Rs." Beers' atlas of 1874 identified the site of the first A.M.E. Zion Church as "M.E. Church. School & Cem."[31]

Esther V.S. Purnell died on April 15, 1905. Her will, on file in the Richmond County Courthouse, is dated April 25, 1902 (Liber 9, Page 278, filed 1905). The date of her death is noted on this document. Her husband is listed as George Purnell. No children of this marriage are listed as beneficiaries, only cousins. Her personal property is listed as $150, and her real estate valued at $75. No obituary of Esther Purnell has been found. George Purnell died on June 23, 1919. His will is found in Liber 24, Page 135, filed 1924. I hope that more information about Esther Purnell will come forth in the future.

DESCENDANTS OF SLAVES

When Sandy Ground began in the 1850s, issues around slavery dominated the political life of this country. In New York State, momentous matters concerning slavery had already been decided. In 1799 children born of slaves were freed by law and in 1827 slavery was entirely abolished. Sandy Ground was settled by free blacks, not runaway slaves. Its early concentration of black families occupying their own living quarters makes it unique on Staten Island.

The A.M.E. Zion denomination nourished many black abolitionist leaders like Frederick Douglass, Harriet Tubman and Sojourner Truth.[32] It has been said by Sandy Ground residents in recent years that there was in Sandy Ground a station on the Underground Railroad, but no early documentation or oral tradition has been found to support this belief.

Like second-generation European immigrants, Sandy Grounders may not have been eager to talk about their origins, but some who had descended from slaves did pass this knowledge on to their children. According to oral family history, Lois Mosley's great-great-grandfather Henry (whose first name has not yet been confirmed by documents) was a slave freed on Staten Island in 1804. George W. Hunter said that his mother, Martha Jennings Hunter (b. 1849), was a runaway slave from Virginia. She settled in Ossining, N.Y., before moving to Sandy Ground in the 1880s.[33] Frank Miles's mother, Adeline Arrikin Miles Robinson (1847-1947), who married first Frank Miles's father and later a Mr. Robinson, was born a slave in Georgia. Her father was a white slaveholder.[34] In the 1940s Bob Green, aged 82, who lived on Sharrott's Road, said his folks were free slaves released by Quakers on the Eastern Maryland shore. They were oystermen on the Chesapeake and they were oystermen here on Prince's Bay.[35]

THE DECLINE OF SANDY GROUND

Sandy Ground as a black community flourished into the first decade of the 20th century but went into economic decline with the closing of Staten Island's oyster beds in 1916. However, many descendants of original settlers continued to live there for several decades. Some, like Lois Mosley, who moved to Mariners Harbor in 1957, began to relocate as better housing on Staten Island became available to African Americans and after the disastrous fire of 1963 destroyed many homes in Sandy Ground. As employment of African Americans in civil service, education and the professions became available, they preferred to relocate elsewhere.

Today, the rapid development of Staten Island's South Shore has transformed Sandy Ground into a white suburb. Its once open fields and woodlands are now occupied by newly built townhouses. Only the Rossville A.M.E. Zion Church and a few early houses remain of the old Sandy Ground. The church is a vital community of approximately 30 families, most of whom commute from other areas of Staten Island or from New Jersey each Sunday to attend services.

NOTES

I would like to thank Nick Dowen for his editorial assistance throughout this essay and this entire volume. Many fine suggestions were given by Dr. Shirley Zavin and Lelia Roberts. Special thanks to Yvonne Taylor for sharing her knowledge of Sandy Ground and for identifying many former residents.

1. Francis Asbury, Methodism's founder in America, made many visits to Westfield, preaching there 19 times from 1771 to 1809. The Woodrow Church was founded in 1787. (Vernon B. Hampton, *Methodist Heritage and Promise on Staten Island.* Staten Island: 1965, p. 7.) Methodists in America historically were against slavery and included African Americans among their members. (William B. McClain, *Black People in the Methodist Church: Whither Thou Goest?* Cambridge, Mass.: Schenkman Publishing Co., 1984, Chapter 3.) Historic church records of the Woodrow Church show no blacks as members. Methodism's acceptance of African Americans as God's children, however, may have influenced property owners' decisions to sell land to blacks in predominately Methodist Westfield. I have no documentation on this matter.

Unfortunately I was unable to locate any primary historical records for the Rossville A.M.E. Zion Church.

2. Hugh Powell, "Prince's Bay, Lemon Creek and the Oyster Industry," an unpublished manuscript [1976], p. 10, in the Black Man of Staten Island (BMOSI) Collection, Staten Island Institute of Arts and Sciences (SIIAS) and Sandy Ground Historical Society (SGHS). I am indebted to Hugh Powell for information on the oyster industry and for his many answers to my questions about Staten Island.

3. Royden Woodward Vosburgh, transcriber and editor, "Records of St. Luke's Protestant Episcopal Church at Rossville...in the former Town of Westfield." Manuscript, 1923, p. 48. SIHS Library.

4. "A New and Correct mapp of the County of Richmond made in the Year 1797 Agreeable to an Act Proposed by the Legislature of the State of New York proposed the 18th day of March 1797." Map 186 filed with the Office of State Engineer and Survey, Albany, New York. Photocopy, SIHS Library.

5. Deeds for the three lots purchased by members of the Purnell family in 1866 exclude timber from the sale. (Liber 76, p. 125; Liber 76, p. 296; and Liber 67, p. 299.) John Jackson's purchase in Liber U, p. 328, recorded June 8, 1831, states, "...all that certain lot of woodland...."

6. Cited in C.W. Leng and W.T. Davis, *Staten Island and its People, A History, 1609-1929.* New York: Lewis Historical Publications, 1930. Vol. I, p. 92.

7. Edwin G. Burrows and Mike Wallace, *Gotham: A History of New York City to 1898.* New York: Oxford University Press, 1999. Chapter 33, "White, Green and Black," is one of several that illuminate in great detail the relationships between the new immigrants and African Americans.

8. The A.M.E. Zion denomination began as a unit of the John Street Methodist Church in Manhattan in 1796, when blacks created their own congregation. At first they depended on white clergy, but in 1822 they established their own denomination with ordained black elders. Zion was the name of their mother church in Manhattan and was chosen as part of their denominational title. (David Henry Bradley, Sr., *A History of the A.M.E. Zion Church, Part I 1796-1872.* Nashville, Tennessee: The Parthenon Press, 1956.)

9. Minna C. Wilkins, "Sandy Ground: A Tiny Racial Island." *Staten Island Historian*, Part I: Jan.-Mar. 1943, pp. 1-3, p. 7. Part II Oct.-Dec. 1943, pp. 25-26, pp. 31-32. Reprinted with an introduction by John B. Woodall in the *Staten Island Historian,* Summer-Fall 1989, pp. 1-10. Wilkins was the first to point out that Sandy Ground was founded by free blacks and that Maryland oystermen were among the early settlers.

10. Liber P, p. 370, recorded Feb. 26, 1828; Liber U, p. 328, recorded June 8, 1831; and Liber 5, p. 32, recorded June 6, 1838. John Jackson's ownership of land on Arthur Kill Road near Kreischerville is the earliest documented purchase in Westfield by a black man. He deserves an honored place in Westfield's African American history. However, I do not consider this action by an individual to be the beginning of the community.

11. Robert L. Schuyler, "Sandy Ground: Archaeological Sampling in a Black Community in Metropolitan New York." Published in *The Conference on Historic Site Archaeology Papers*, Vol. 7, pp. 13-52. Columbia, S.C., University of South Carolina, 1972. Appendix 1, pp. 45-48, is an invaluable listing of the gravestone inscriptions in the Rossville A.M.E. Zion Church cemetery.

12. Wilkins gives the names of the oyster sloops owned by Sandy Ground's prominent residents. Mr. Hunter in Joseph Mitchell's article (1956) and William "Pop" Pedro in the National Register project (1980) follow suit. It may be that Henry purchased the *Fanny Fern* from Dawson Landin and his brother Robert Landin (Askins, 1988, p. 108).

13. William Askins, "The Sandy Ground Survey Project: Archaeologi-

cal and Historical Research in Support of a National Register Nomination." Unpublished, unpaginated manuscript in BMOSI Collection, 1980.

This survey, sponsored by the Sandy Ground Historical Society, was conducted from July 9 to August 23, 1979. Shovel tests and walkovers throughout the community were conducted and the results analyzed. The survey proposed the boundaries of the Sandy Ground Historic Archaeological National Register District, which was created in 1982.

The oral history of William "Pop" Pedro conducted by members of the project team was especially valuable to my research, as well as the identification of buildings and building sites.

Askins's 1988 Ph.D. dissertation is titled "Sandy Ground: Historical Archaeology of Class and Ethnicity in a Nineteenth Century Community on Staten Island." Chapter 3 deals in detail with Sandy Ground oystermen and the larger industry (pp. 91f) and with Sandy Ground's race relations (pp. 117f). It is available from Proquest Information and Learning, P.O. Box 1346, Ann Arbor, Michigan 48106-1346.

14. Gorton Carruth, *The Encyclopedia of American Facts & Dates.* Eighth Edition. New York: Harper & Row, 1987, p. 248.

15. Kenneth T. Jackson, ed., *The Encyclopedia of New York City.* New Haven: Yale University Press, 1995, p. 836.

16. A. Y. Hubbell, *History of Methodism and the Methodist Churches of Staten Island, New York.* New York: Richmond Publishing Co., 1898, p. 149.

17. Bishop J. W. Hood, *One Hundred Years of the African Methodist Episcopal Zion Church: The Centennial of African Methodism.* New York: A.M.E. Zion Book Concern, 1895, p. 82 and p. 94. Microfiche at the Schomburg Center, New York Public Library.

18. Wilkins (1989), p. 7.

19. Hubbell, p. 151.

20. W. S. Webb, comp., *Webb's Consolidated Directory of the North and South Shores, Staten Island, 1890-91.* Copy in the Staten Island Historical Society Library.

21. William T. Davis, "Staten Island Names: Ye Olde Names and Nicknames." *Proceedings of the Natural Science Association of Staten Island,* March 14, 1896, p. 76.

22. Joseph Post, Silas Harris's son-in-law, and Joseph Tupe are also buried in Plot 180. Many thanks to Dora Arslanian, president of the Silver Mount Cemetery, and to Carol Berardi, a Board member, for providing me with photocopies of the original purchase records. We were unable to locate the actual gravesites.

23. James M. Wright, *The Free Negro in Maryland, 1634-1890*. New York: Octagon Books, 1971 (reprint of 1921 edition). Chapter 10, "Attempt to Check the Growth of Free Negro Population," refers to Liberia. This work was cited by Minna Wilkins.

24. Joseph Mitchell's notes in the BMOSI Collection at SIIAS and SGHS. These notes on Sandy Ground's residents and their history were compiled from 1947 to 1955.

25. Joseph Mitchell, "Mr. Hunter's Grave." *The New Yorker,* Sept. 22, 1956, pp. 50f. This article is exemplary as a work of local history. It should be read by everyone interested in Sandy Ground. Mr. Mitchell's notes, cited in Note 24, include many interviews not used in the published article.

26. Askins, oral history interview with William "Pop" Pedro in "The Sandy Ground Survey Project."

27. Mitchell, "Mr. Hunter's Grave."

28. Askins, oral history interview with William "Pop" Pedro in "The Sandy Ground Survey Project."

29. Wilkins (1989), p. 6.

30. "Esther Purnell was pioneer in education." *Staten Island Advance*, March 27, 1986, clipping in SIHS Library file.

31. The word "school" appears on Dripp's Map of 1850 on the north side of Woodrow Road. It is seen on none of the later maps or atlases. An undated photograph bearing the caption "Sandy Ground School" now in the Staten Island Historical Society collection shows a 19th-century clapboard residence. This photograph was probably taken in the 1920s or 1930s, long after Esther Purnell's death. It may have been marked thus because of the 1850 map.

32. David Henry Bradley, Sr., *A History of the A.M.E. Zion Church. Part I, 1796-1872.* Nashville, Tenn.: The Parthenon Press, 1956. Collection of Yvonne Taylor.

33. Mitchell, "Mr. Hunter's Grave."

34. Telephone interview with Josephine Berry, great-granddaughter of Adeline Arrikin Miles Robinson, by Barnett Shepherd. Aug. 2001.

35. Meyer Berger, "About New York," ca. 1940. Unidentified clipping in verticle file at SIHS.

CENSUS SOURCES

Basic information about Sandy Ground's residents has been provided by Staten Island census records for Westfield. These records are available on Staten Island on microfilm at SIHS and SIIAS. Indexes of Federal censuses from 1790 through 1870 are available at SIHS.

Three publications by Borough Historian Richard Dickenson about African Americans were especially helpful. They are:

1. *Census Occupations of Afro-American Families on Staten Island, 1840-1875*. Staten Island, N.Y.: Staten Island Institute of Arts and Sciences, 1981. 117 pp. This book includes an essay titled "Censuses: Origins, Causes and Means" and reproduces the texts of the 1799 Act freeing children of slaves and the 1817 Act that abolished slavery in New York State in 1827.

2. "1875: Afro-American Households in Richmond County (Staten Island), State of New York." Afro-American Abstracts #12. Sandy Ground Historical Society, 1983. This is a listing of African American households from the New York State Census of 1875.

3. *Afro-American Vital Records and 20th Century Abstracts: Richmond County/Staten Island, 1915 and 1925, New York State Census Records*. Sandy Ground Historical Society, 1985. 194 pp. "Census Notes" and "The Demise of the N.Y. State Census" provide a history of the New York State censuses.

THE BLACK MAN
ON STATEN ISLAND COLLECTION

The Black Man on Staten Island Collection (BMOSI) was utilized by me at SIIAS, whose Archivist/Researcher, Dorothy A. D'Eletto, was most helpful. This collection was begun in 1973 by SIIAS Librarian Gail Schneider and was enlarged by many others subsequently. It was transferred in 1997 to the Sandy Ground Historical Society, where it is maintained with other African American collections. These collections are described in the *Catalog Guide to the Archives of the Sandy Ground Historical Society Library/Museum* (SGHS, 1998). Information: Sandy Ground Historical Society, 1538 Woodrow Road, Staten Island, N.Y. 10309. Telephone: 718-317-5796.

Area Maps and Photographs

"Outline & Index Map of the Borough of Richmond,
City of New York, 1898" in *Atlas of the Borough of Richmond,
City of New York.* New York: E. Robinson, 1898.

Sandy Ground is not named on this map. I have circled the intersection of Woodrow Road with Bloomingdale Road (leading into Pleasant Avenue) as being its geographical center.

What had been Westfield is here named Ward 5. The township form of government was dropped on Jan. 1, 1898, upon Staten Island's consolidation with New York City.

To the *north* of Sandy Ground about two miles away lies Rossville, located on the Arthur Kill, here called "Staten Island Sound." To the *east* on Woodrow Road stands the Woodrow Methodist Church, the largest, most important church in the area. Although the area is called Woodrow, there was no village of that name. To the *south* about two miles away is Pleasant Plains, a town that came into being with the opening of the Staten Island Railroad in 1860. Another two miles south lies Prince's Bay. It was the scene of oystering, the area's major industry. One mile *west* of Sandy Ground on Sharrott's Road is Kreischerville (Charleston). By 1898, Tottenville at the western end of the Staten Island Railroad had become the area's largest town. From Tottenville a ferry carried passengers to Perth Amboy.

The towns that surrounded Sandy Ground were for whites only. However, white families did live in Sandy Ground.

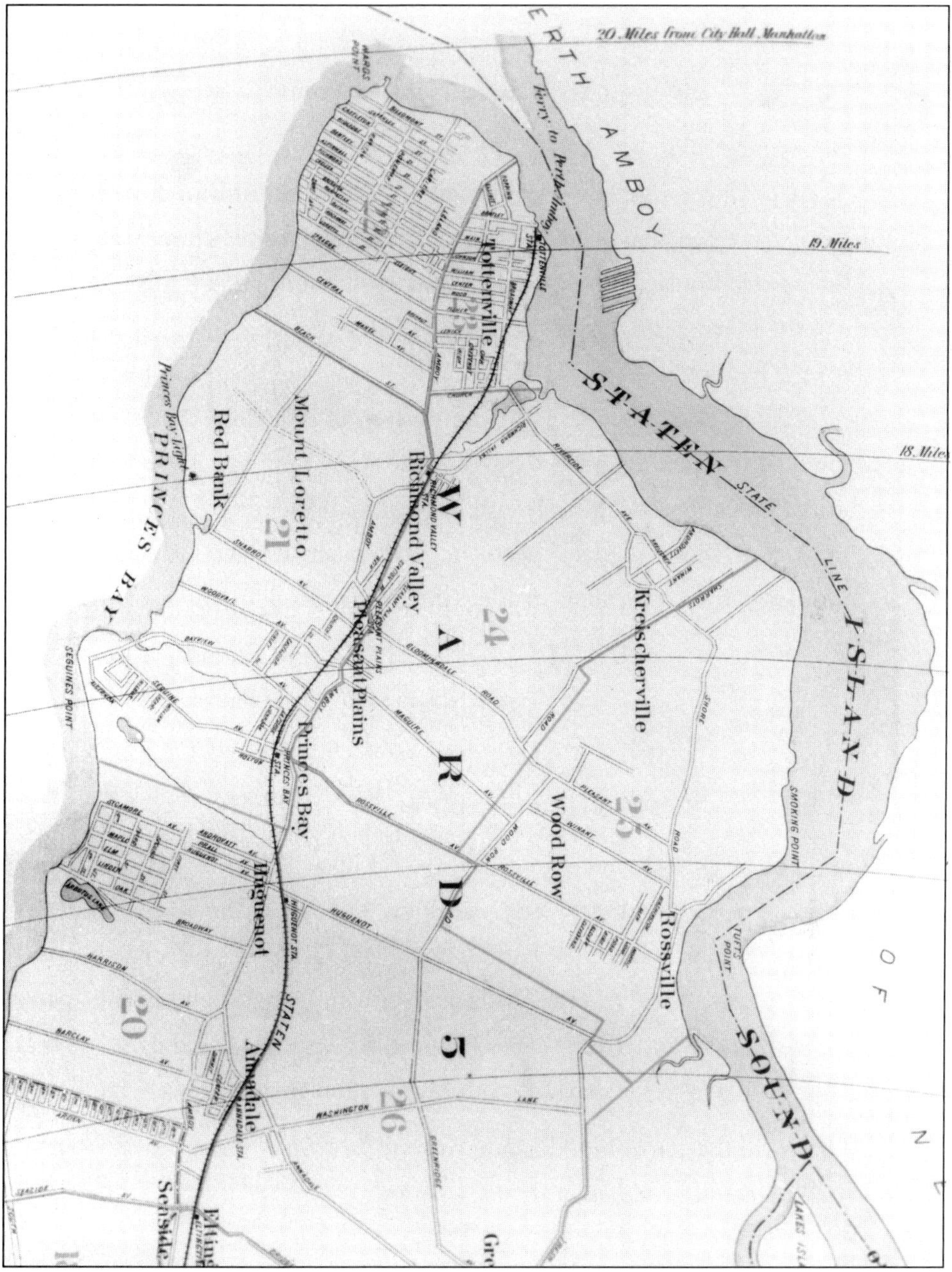
20 Miles from City Hall, Manhattan
19 Miles
18 Miles
PERTH AMBOY
Ferry to Perth Amboy
STATEN ISLAND
STATE LINE
SOUND
WARDS POINT
Tottenville
Richmond Valley
Mount Loretto
Red Bank
Princes Bay Light
PRINCES BAY
SEGUINES POINT
WARD 5
21
24
25
20
26
Kreischerville
Pleasant Plains
Princes Bay
Wood Row
Rossville
Huguenot
Annadale
SMOKING POINT
TUFTS POINT

"Bloomingdale Road, Sandy Ground"

Photographer unknown. Ca. 1930. Staten Island Historical Society (SIHS). Looking south. From left to right on the eastern side of the road can be seen the two "baymen's cottages," Grandma Cooper's house, and the Prasse farmhouse. The oystermen walked four miles down this road early in the morning to their boats on Prince's Bay.

For the children the gradual slope of Bloomingdale Road southward provided ideal snow sledding. At the bottom of this slope was "The Hollow," where the trees arched tall over the street, setting a frightening nighttime scene for Lois Mosley and her girlhood friends.

The name "Bloomingdale," according to William T. Davis, originated as an old name for the valley at Pleasant Plains through which Sandy Brook flows.

"Ice Pond, South Side of the Road"

Photograph by Percy L. Sperr, Sept. 23, 1927. Milstein Division of United States History, Local History & Genealogy, The New York Public Library, Astor, Lenox and Tilden Foundations. 1253 B10. The picturesque scene reveals the beauty of the landscape surrounding Sandy Ground. Open fields and wooded areas are visible atop gently sloping hills.

This property was owned by white families, first by the Neilsen family (1898 and 1907 atlases) and later by Gustaf Fagerhund (1917 atlas). The buildings fronted on Sharrott's Road a short distance from Lois Mosley's Landin grandparents' house.

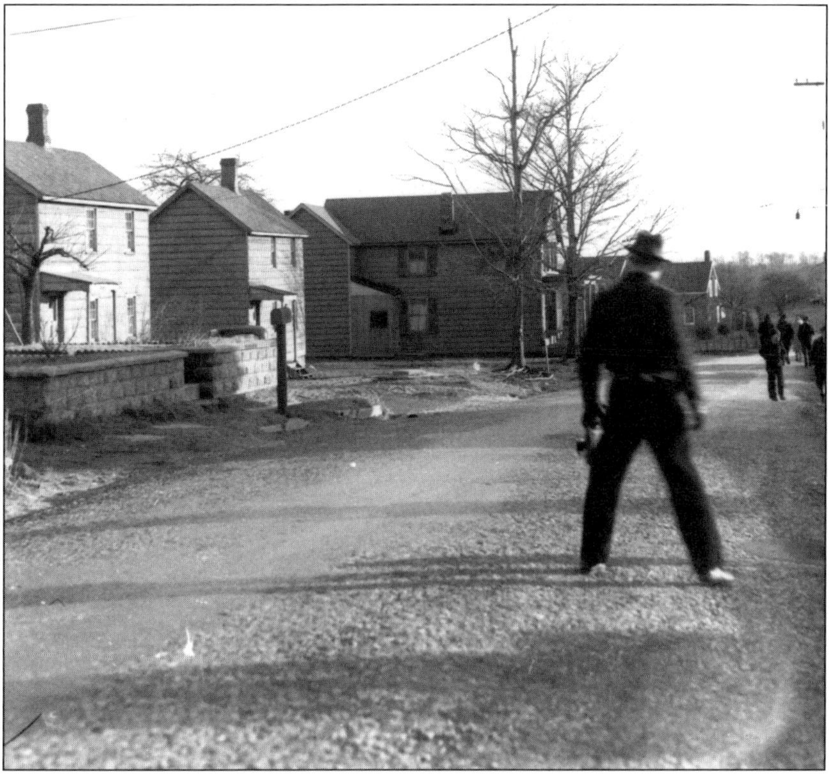

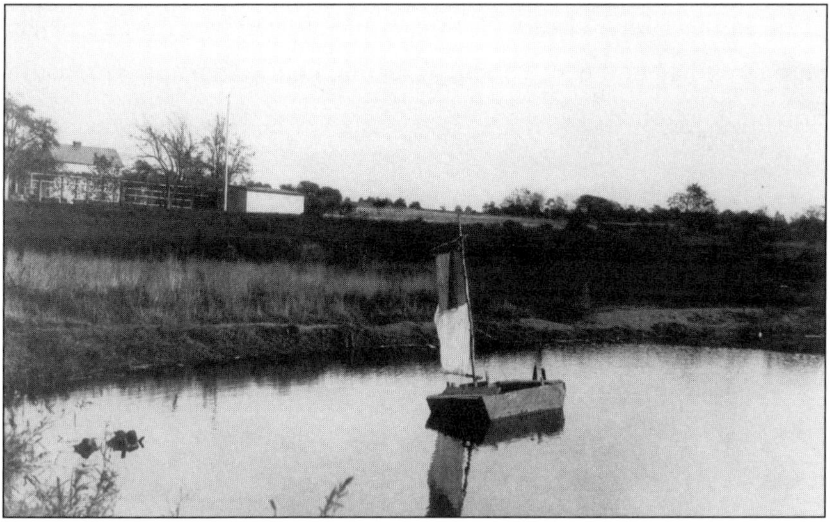

"Sharrott's Road, Sandy Ground, Staten Island"

Postcard. Photograph by W. J. Grimshaw. Ca. 1905-1925. SIHS. Here African American farm workers pause for the photographer while harvesting corn, probably to be loaded onto the wagon.

"Staten Islanders"

Photograph by F. M. Simonson. Ca. 1906. SIHS. These African Americans may be from Sandy Ground, although the precise location is not given. In the 19th and early 20th centuries Staten Island was a major supplier of hay to the metropolitan region. Oxen often appear in early farm photographs.

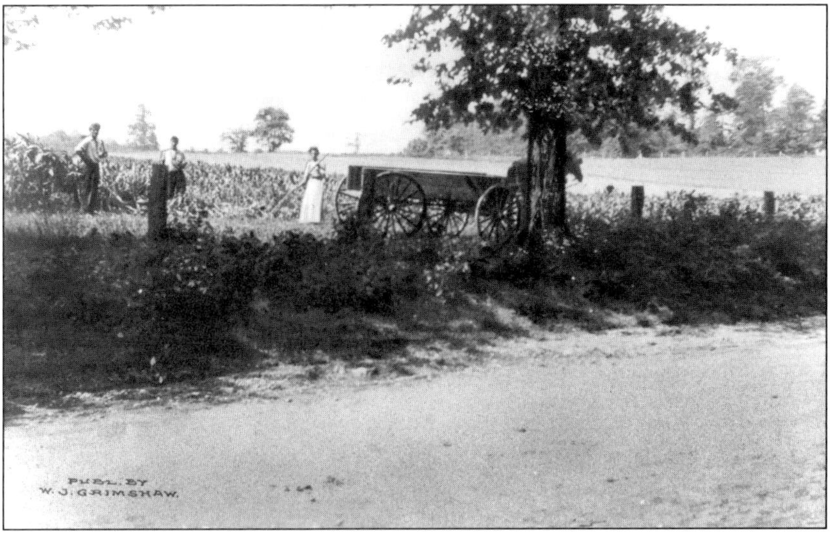
PUBL. BY
W. J. GRIMSHAW.

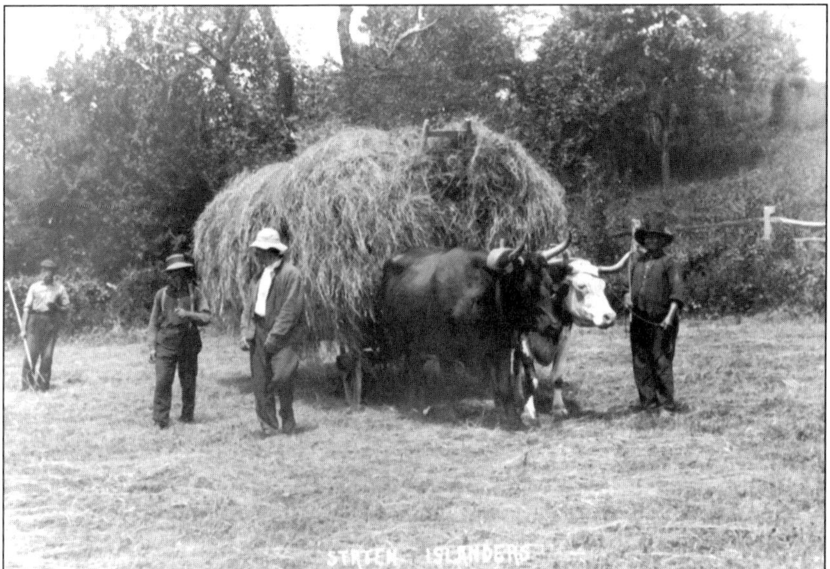
STATEN ISLANDERS

"Woodrow Church, S.I."

Postcard. Photographer unknown. Ca. 1900. SIHS. This imposing Greek Revival church was built in 1842, replacing an earlier church. The Italianate bell tower was added in the 1870s. The thick woods seen in this photograph illustrate the name "Woodrow." The church and the large graveyard (which contains many 18th-century gravestones) indicate the long-standing importance of Methodism in Westfield.

African Americans never became members of this church.

"Rossville Seen from Rossville Bay"

Photograph by W. J. Grimshaw. Ca. 1905. SIHS. Already showing signs of decline, this small waterfront town is still beautiful. The large Greek Revival residence on the left was built by Joseph H. Seguine, Westfield's largest farmer. In the center nearly hidden by a tall tree is the small, but elegant Gothic-towered St. Luke's Episcopal Church, built in 1844. Early Sandy Ground residents Silas Harris and his wife Ann were communicants. A side view of the Methodist Chapel is to the right.

Not visible here is "Ross Castle," the most extraordinary residence in Rossville. It was built by Col. William E. Ross, a hero of the War of 1812. Blazing Star, the old name of the village, was changed to Rossville in his honor.

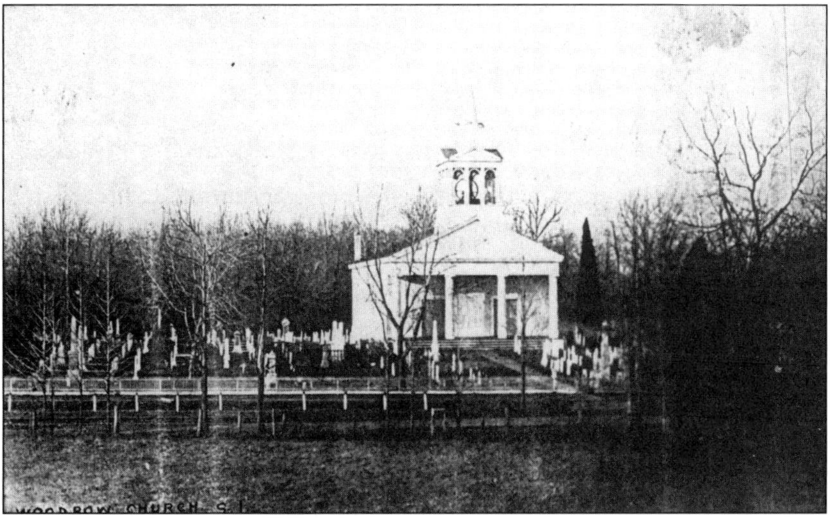
WOODROW CHURCH, S.I.

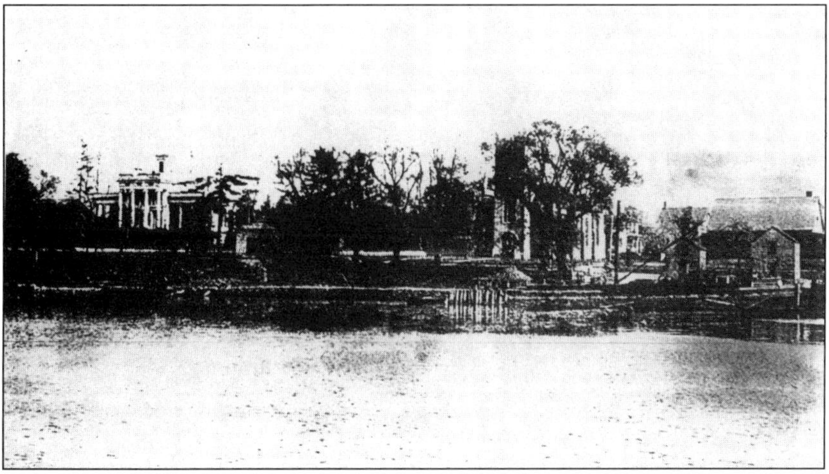

"Amboy Road, Pleasant Plains"

Postcard. Photograph by W. J. Grimshaw. Ca. 1910. SIHS. Pleasant Plains, with its commercial buildings fronting on Amboy Road, became the shopping area for most Sandy Ground residents. Bloomingdale Road can be seen at the top of the street coming down from the left. The railroad crossing sign is prominent on the left, as is the Western Union Telegraph sign. In the 1920s and 1930s many Sandy Ground women worked as domestics in the white households of Pleasant Plains.

"Kreischerville"

Photograph by William Guether. Date unknown. SIHS. Its neat workers' residences were inhabited largely by German-Americans. The brick factory, whose tall chimneys appear in the background, was on the shore of the Arthur Kill.

Sandy Grounders had little or no contact with this community. Today it is called Charleston.

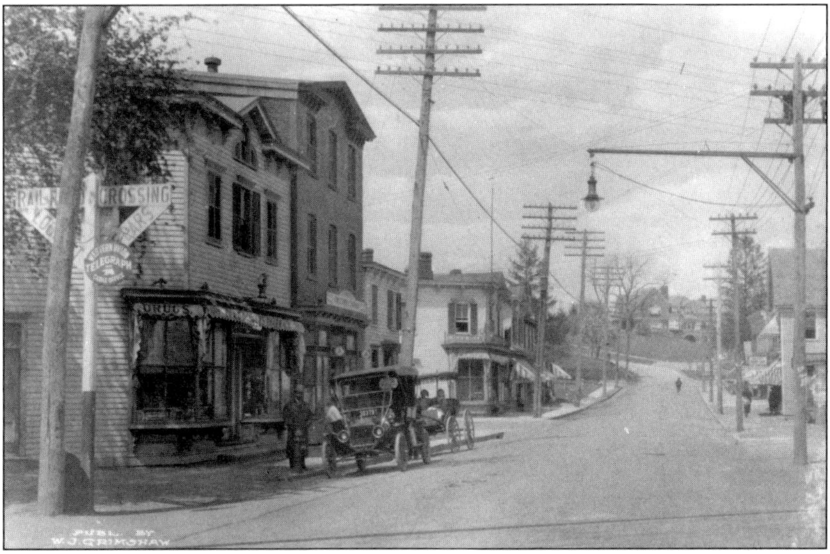
CROSSING
TELEGRAPH
DRUGS
PUBL. BY
W.J. GRIMSHAW

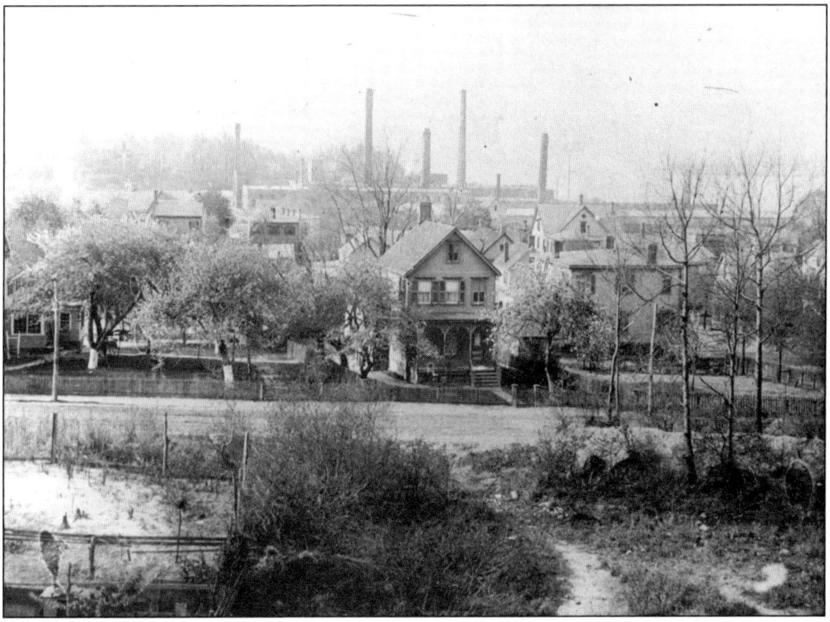

"Famous Oyster Location.—View of Prince's Bay"

Illustrated News, July 16, 1853, p. 20. From the Collection of the_ Staten Island Institute of Arts & Sciences, New York (SIIAS). This scene from the heights of Red Bank with its lighthouse shows Prince's Bay and Staten Island's southern shoreline, with the Atlantic Ocean in the distance. Stakes in the water of Prince's Bay mark the oystermen's seed beds.

"The Oyster Business—Raking for Oysters"

Illustrated News, July 16, 1853, p. 20. SIIAS. The men are holding the long-handled tongs that gathered the oysters from the bottom of the bay and deposited them in the boat. Oystering was hard work. The boat is a "Staten Island skiff," especially designed for oyster work. One of these skiffs is on display in the Historical Museum at Historic Richmond Town, together with appropriate tools.

FAMOUS OYSTER LOCALITY.—VIEW OF PRINCE'S BAY,

ILLUSTRATED NEWS.   [JULY 16, 18

THE OYSTER BUSINESS—RAKING FOR OYSTERS.

"Oystering at Prince's Bay."

Oil painting by Alex Matthew. SIHS. This painting is a copy on canvas of the previous illustration. The poles marking the oyster beds' boundaries are emphasized here. This painting reminds me of the dramatic death of Lois Mosley's much-admired great-grandfather, Dawson Landin. His brief obituary appears in the *Richmond County Advance,* Feb. 25, 1899:

DIED SUDDENLY

Dawson Landon (colored), aged 73 years, of Kreischerville, died suddenly in his boat Tuesday morning. Landon was an oysterman, and went in his skiff Tuesday morning with a companion to work. While tonging oysters he was taken suddenly ill and died before he reached the shore. Coroner Seaver was notified and took charge of the remains.

"The Oyster Business—Dredging for Oysters."

Illustrated News, July 16, 1853, p. 20. SIIAS. This small single-masted sailing vessel was called a sloop. The workers are shown pulling in the dredging bag whose contents will be dumped into the boat. These sloops were used for a variety of tasks, including taking oysters to market. Dawson Landin owned the *Pacific,* a 40-footer. Francis Henry owned the *Fanny Fern* and Robert H. Landin the *Independence,* both 30-footers.

"Tottenville, Staten Island, Sept. 6, 1924."

Photograph by William T. Davis. SIIAS, Davis Collection, No. 3651. This shows an abandoned oyster float on the beach. Such floats were used to prepare the oysters for market. Oysters were loaded onto these floats and submerged in shallow freshwater streams (like Lemon Creek, which flows into Prince's Bay) to cleanse themselves of salt water.

"Annapolis. Darkies opening oysters. Fine day.
Skylight, dark. 10 a.m., Tuesday, Sept. 25, 1894.
Stanley 50, Waterbury lense, 10 secs. 50 ft."

Photograph by Alice Austen. SIHS. Though not taken on Staten Island, this haunting photograph shows the employment of black men (apparently under a white supervisor) in the labor-intensive oyster business.

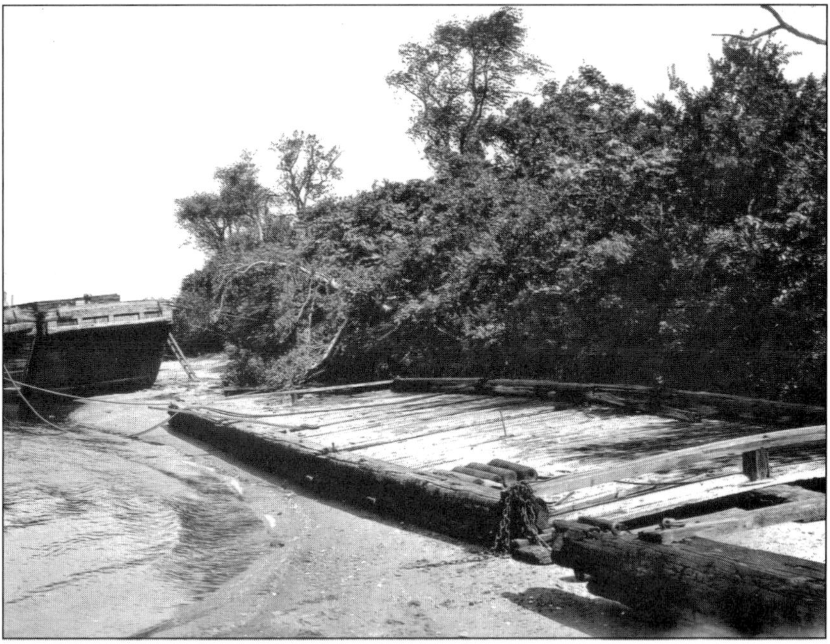

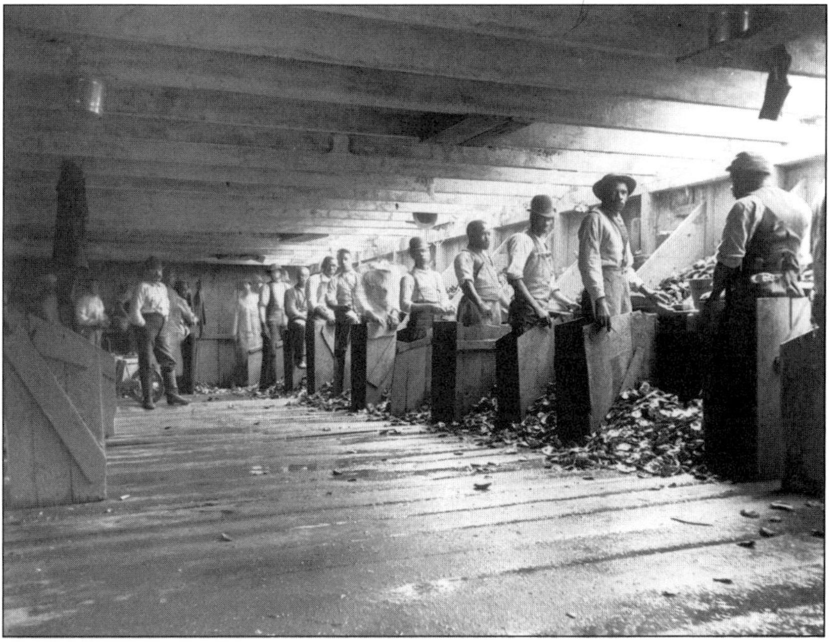

Atlas of the Borough of Richmond, City of New York.

New York: E. Robinson, 1898. Portions of Plates 24 and 25. These detailed maps with property lines show the ownership of land in Sandy Ground.

North of the intersection of Woodrow Road and Bloomingdale Road appears the original Rossville A.M.E. Zion Church property (1) with the outline of the original church building. It fronts on an unnamed street, today's Crabtree Avenue. This is the location of the present church cemetery.

To the north are three lots marked "Harris," which were the core of the early community, called "Harrisville."

North of the Harris lots are two non-contiguous lots, one denominated "Mt. Zion Church" (2), and the other "Church Prop." (3) today termed the "Poor Cemetery."

On Bloomingdale Road south of Woodrow Road is found the "Methodist Church" lot (4). This is the present-day Rossville A.M.E. Zion Church.

Robt. Landon and D. Landon lots appear on the north side of Sharrott's Road. On the south side are two Cutting family lots. On Bloomingdale Road just north of the Sharrott's Road intersection is seen the W. H. Hinds property, which became the Prasse farm. South of the intersection is seen the Isaac Harris property.

G. C. Graves 8 A.
Ellen M. Graham 4 A.
Mrs. Charlotte Mosely
Mrs. Skinner
Isaac Wort
15 A.
Henry I. Mason
62 A.
Bloomingdale Road
Woodrow Road
WOOD ROW
Sharrott's Road
John Purnell
Jas. Guyon
Gruber
Geo. Purnell
John Tyler
Jas. Finney
W. H. Hinds
W. B. Sharrot
T. F. Oechsli
C. Bogardus 4 A.
Isaac Harris
Jos. Post 3 A.
James S. Guyon
18 A.
Philip Clarius
A. Winant
Kaolin Co.
Mrs. John Cutting
Bishop
Tupes
Mrs. Post
Jos. Riggs
Jas. A. Reed

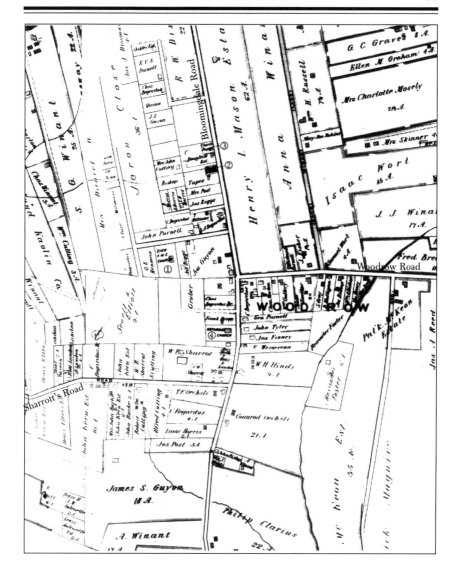

*Staten Island Business Register and Railroad
and Steamboat Guide, 1879-80.*

SIHS. Title page with advertisement. Bogardus' Corner, the intersection of Woodrow Road and Bloomingdale Road, was an early name for Sandy Ground. The C. Bogardus & Son grocery and feed store was located there. It included two businesses requiring ice, ice cream manufacturing and undertaking.

STATEN ISLAND

BUSINESS REGISTER

AND

RAILROAD AND STEAMBOAT GUIDE,

1879-'80.

ANNADALE, see also SEA SIDE.

BUTCHER.

McFARLAND W. A, Beef, lamb, mutton, veal, poultry and game in season.

HOTEL.

ANNADALE HOUSE, Francis Murphy

LAWYER.

HEDLEY JOHN H. 59 Nassau, N. Y.

PAINTER.

GILBY JAMES.

BOGARDUS' CORNER.

BUTCHERS.

GUYON JAMES S.
Sharott Winant B.

GENERAL STORE.

BOGARDUS C. & SON. See ice cream and undertakers.

ICE CREAM MANUFACTURERS.

BOGARDUS C. & SON, see Undertakers.

UNDERTAKERS.

BOGARDUS C. & SON, see ice cream.

C. BOGARDUS & SON,

GROCERIES, FLOUR AND FEED,

AND

ICE CREAM MANUFACTURERS,

AND FURNISHING UNDERTAKERS,

BOGARDUS' CORNER, STATEN ISLAND

One mile from from Pleasant Station, S. I. R. R.

Bodies laid out and iced at all hours, Day and Night, in the Patent Corpse Preserver. Hearse and Carriages furnished and Funerals attended at shortest notice.

P. O. Address Rossville, S. I.

"New York.—The Late Strawberry Crop.—Sunday Morning
Pickers at Rossville, Staten Island."

Leslie's Weekly, June 28, 1884, p. 298. General Research Division, The
New York Public Library, Astor, Lenox and Tilden Foundations. A brief
article accompanying this illustration states that these pickers were paid.
None appears to be black. Lois Mosley notes that Sandy Ground's soil
was good for growing strawberries, as do George Hunter and William
"Pop" Pedro.

"Uncle Harry Hicks and his Wife Aunt Mary."

Photographer and date unknown. SIHS. The 1875 Census for Westfield
lists Harry Hicks, aged 62, oysterman, born King's County, and Maria
Hicks, aged 66, born Richmond County. It is said that they drove this
wagon through Prince's Bay and Pleasant Plains for years. The
photograph shows an intriguing assortment of containers by the door,
but we do not know if this was their house, or if they lived in Sandy
Ground.

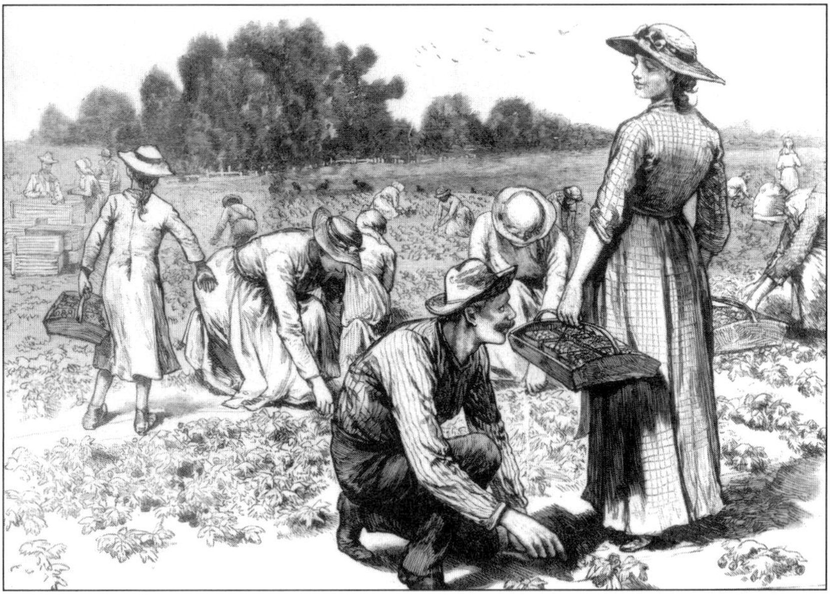

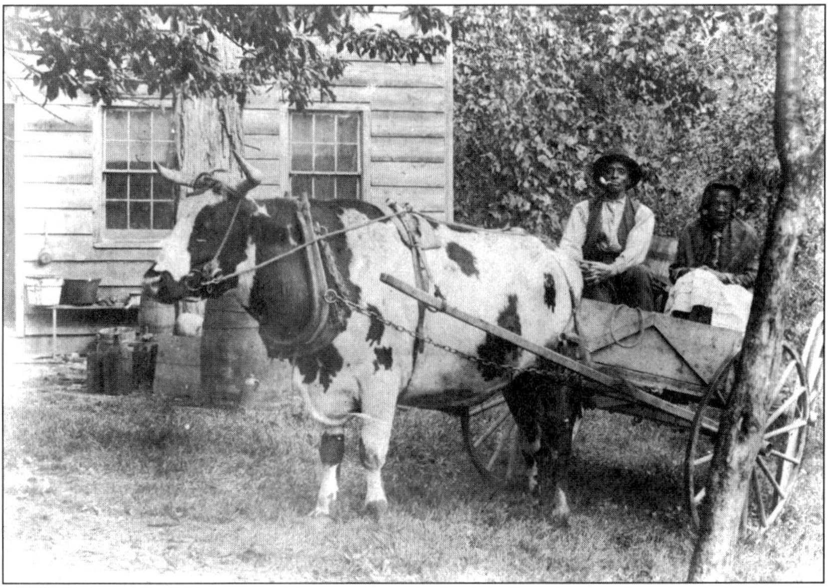

"Alfred Cutting House."

Photographer unknown, ca. 1900. SIHS. E. Robinson's atlas, 1907, Plate 24, identifies this property on the south side of Sharrott's Road, just beyond the corner of Bloomingdale Road (behind what later became Reinhardt's) as "Alfred Cutting 4 ac." Alfred Cutting (1820-1910), with his white beard, stands on the left. The woman in the center may be his wife, Mary Ann Pollicut Cutting (d. 1905), and on the right one of his two daughters.

    Cutting was born in Suffolk, England. His father immigrated to New York in 1823, settling in the Williamsburg section of Brooklyn. Alfred moved to the Rossville area in 1840, after his father's death. In 1862 he rented "a house and garden lot" on Woodrow Road and in 1873 purchased a four-acre lot on Sharrott's Road, which became the family homestead pictured here (Leng and Davis, Vol. III, p. 322). He was a successful truck farmer and also hired himself out to others. SIHS has a daily journal kept by him in the 1890s. After Alfred's death this property was owned by his son, Stephen L. Cutting.

"Robert Cutting House."

Photographer unknown, ca. 1900. SIHS. This is the Sharrott's Road home of Robert J. Cutting, oldest son (b. 1855) of Alfred and Mary Ann Cutting. He occupied a 3.2-acre lot adjoining the west side of his father's property (1907 atlas). The driver of the horsedrawn vehicle is not identified nor are the other persons, although two of the women appear in the previous photograph.

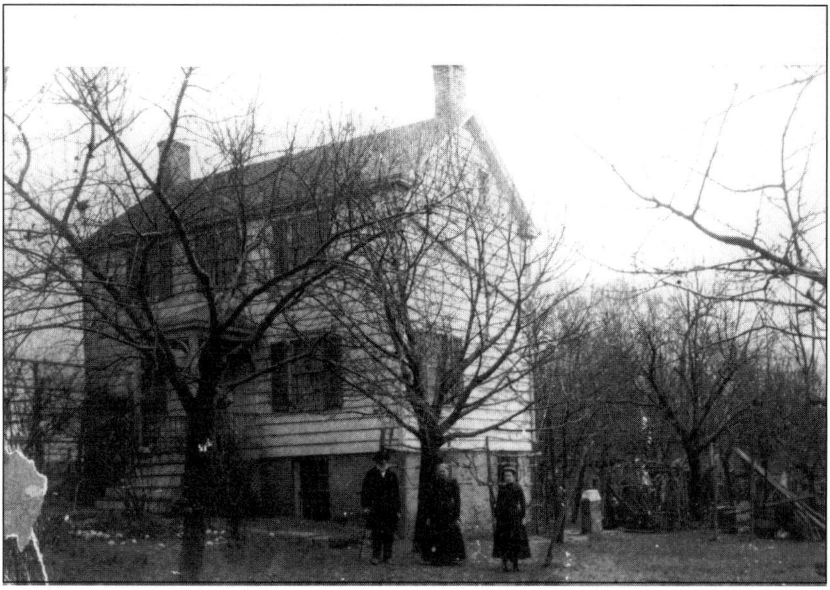

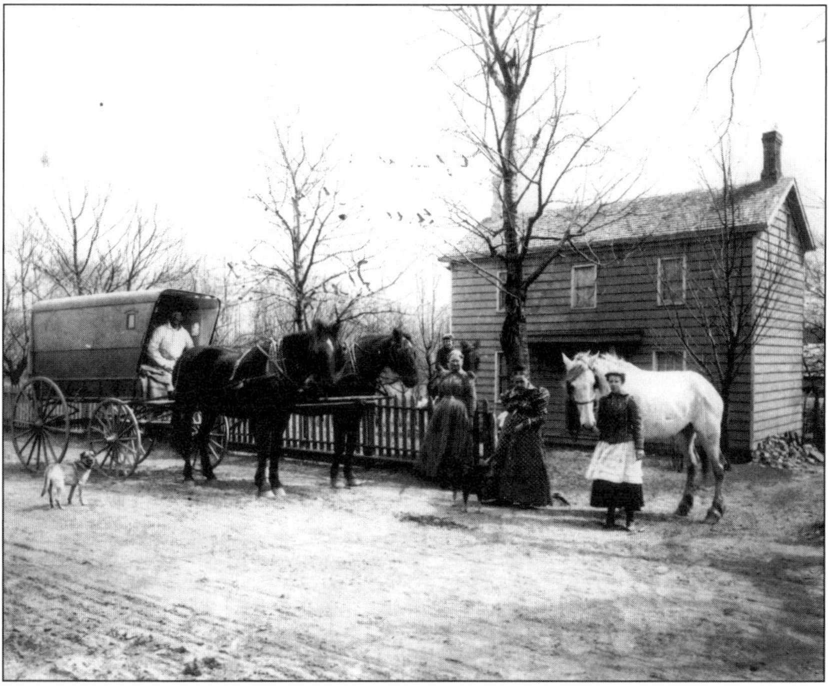

PART TWO

Sandy Ground Memories
of Lois A. H. Mosley

Sandy Ground Memories

INTRODUCTION

I FIRST began to write down my many memories while I was in the
hospital recovering from surgery in 1988. I was determined not to
lose track of my family history so that my children, grandchildren and
great-grandchildren could appreciate their family's roots and the extraordinary lives we experienced in Sandy Ground. Although we did not know
it, in my childhood our family and most Sandy Ground families were
poor, but we were part of a unified group that few communities could
equal.

The Rossville A.M.E. Zion Church has always been the center of our
community. My family has been involved with the church from its beginning in 1850 right up to the present. Church members have encouraged
me to write down my memories, while providing much emotional support for this project. Several have contributed their own chapters.

The devastating fire of 1963 destroyed my maternal Henry grandparents' home as well as other houses. The Westshore Expressway now
runs through the area where once stood my maternal Landin grandparents' house. Many Sandy Ground residents suffered similar losses. The
developers who acquired land here in recent years are indifferent to the
history of Sandy Ground. The physical destruction of the community
which I have witnessed has increased the urgency of my desire to record
my memories of it.

Essays about Sandy Ground have been published by the Sandy
Ground Historical Society, of which I am an original member. Those
essays, as well as articles in newspapers and magazines about Esther V.S.

Purnell, Isaac Harris, George Hunter, William "Pop" Pedro, and many others are very important, but do not give enough credit to the women of Sandy Ground. I know they were "the power behind the throne." I want to tell their stories, too.

Let me add that Sandy Ground could give Peyton Place a run for its money, as many a small town can verify. In Sandy Ground you did not dare fall too deeply in love with anyone before you checked them out. You might find yourself in love with your cousin, your aunt or uncle, or even your half-brother or sister. This has seldom been written down.

Many thanks to the people who helped me remember the good times and the interesting times we had in Sandy Ground. Without their help *Sandy Ground Memories* would be incomplete. Many thanks also to those who wrote their own family stories published here: Thelma Pedro, Marie Moody Bowers, Mildred Harris Allen, Norma Wallen McGhie, Maude Landin and Malvina Moody Temple. Others who shared their family memories with me are mentioned in the text. Gregory and Elena Mosley, my son and daughter-in-law, have my gratitude for urging me to persevere. I would like to thank the typists who succeeded in making heads and tails out of my rememberings: Rowena Hemingway, Robin Rimpson, Sharon Mortenson, Anita Cobbs-Haynes, and Linda Ganzy. Special thanks to my daughter Gloria.

Most especially I would like to thank Barnett Shepherd, Executive Director of the Staten Island Historical Society from 1981 to 2000. Upon his retirement he volunteered his time and expertise to help shape my memories into book form for future publication. He spent many months reviewing, clarifying, and encouraging me to say more about nearly every topic.

I was born on Nov. 17, 1926, and lived in Sandy Ground, this hamlet in southwestern Staten Island, until I moved to the Mariners Harbor Houses in 1957. I stayed in close contact with Sandy Ground and continued to feel my real home was there. Even after moving to New Jersey in 1975, I still come back to attend church every Sunday, and take part in other community activities during the week. Three generations of my family are buried in the A.M.E. Zion Church graveyard.

In my mind Sandy Ground will always remain my true home. I hope you will enjoy reading about the remarkable people who once lived there.

FAMILY

My first recollection of home is the family house, pink, that was next door to the Rossville A.M.E. Zion Church. This was 570 Bloomingdale Road. I lived there with my mother and father, my brother Howard, and sisters Mary Emily and Frances Helen. It was a tall house and Mr. Buster Moody, Mother's cousin, and Miss Olive, William "Pop" Pedro's daughter, lived with us when they first married.

Sandy Ground was our neighborhood. It included our church and school and nearby were my grandparents, aunts, uncles, and many cousins. We lived briefly at 570, then moved to Grandmother Henry's house at 548 Bloomingdale Road. Aunt Jo, Grandfather Landin's sister, lived on the top floor. We later moved across the street to 569 rear Bloomingdale Road, one of three houses managed by Mr. Hunter.

MOTHER

My mother was Susan Ann Landin Henry. Both of us were born at Richmond Memorial Hospital and grew up in Sandy Ground. Her parents' home was 187 Sharrott's Road. Outside my family she was fondly called "Aunt Sue" or "Aunt Susie" by all who knew her. Everyone in our neighborhood was welcome at "Aunt Susie's house." She was fun-loving; she played games with us children and even taught all of us how to play pinochle! She was very talented and a wonderful mother.

Musician   She was the church organist and choir director at the Rossville A.M.E. Zion Church for many years. As a girl she had taken piano lessons from a Mrs. Wilbur in Pleasant Plains and also studied with Aunt Gert Landin. She later played the piano with my father's band at Saturday night dances in New Jersey.

Cook   Mother was famous for her apple dumplings. Every weekend she made a big batch together with her famous white sauce and would sell them on Saturdays to benefit the church. Her dumplings sold for 15 or 20 cents apiece. If you didn't have the money, "Buy now and pay

Church conference participants, ca. 1935. *Left to right: Susan Ann Henry, Lois's mother; The Rev. A. P. Jenkins, Rossville A.M.E. Zion pastor; Mrs. Jenkins; Frances Landin; Bertha Wallen; Gertrude Landin. This is the only known photograph of Lois's mother.*

later." For dinner every Sunday we had ham, potato salad and chocolate pudding. I have never been able to make chocolate pudding like my mother's, so I use the prepared mix.

Hairdresser   Even though she wasn't a professional, my mother was also the town hairdresser. When we had our hair done for special occasions such as Christmas, Easter, Children's Day, birthdays and a few other holidays, "Aunt Susie" was busy. She charged 25 cents.

"Doctor"   When we were ill "Doctor Susie" always had a home remedy. There was always a cure. I know the young people today are impressed by modern medicine. That is not to say our mother's remedies did not work and would not be effective today. For a chest cold, if Vicks and Vaseline didn't work, maybe Father John's Cough Syrup would. Cod liver oil was given to us, two tablespoons to a tablespoon of Vicks (by mouth) in the morning before we went to school. That was nasty!

For whooping cough, mother would take dry mustard and water and make a mixture and spread it on a diaper. Then you went to bed and burned to death all night. If you had a sore throat, five percent iodine or Argyrol was painted on your palate. If you didn't gag during the procedure, you could consider yourself cured.

For the croup a favorite standby was a teaspoonful of sugar with three drops of kerosene on top. Sulfur and molasses were given at the end of the winter to clear our blood. Sugar was used for many other cures. One that I remember is a paste of Octagon soap and sugar that was applied to boils. Boils used to come in the wrong places and made it difficult to sit down. The soap and sugar were made into a paste and applied to our boils. When children have ringworm today, they are treated with gentian violet liquid. Our parents would soak copper pennies in vinegar and apply the penny to the white spot. Sometimes they used plain old ink. We were cured.

When I was 12 years old, Father left Mother. She had to raise four children on her own and she did. We went on welfare which helped with our groceries. Recipients had to go to Pleasant Plains under the railroad station to pick up their food. We had to go daily to pick up milk. At times we received powdered milk (ugh), canned stew meat, mutton, white margarine with the orange powder that had to be mixed in a bowl, grains and surplus food. How lucky we were when they gave us prunes and raisins! The kids would walk around with a pocketful of raisins, sometimes using them as missiles.

Her Night Out   Wednesday nights Mother would always go to the Stadium Treater in Tottenville. Aunt Helen, Father's sister, drove Aunt Bea, Aunt Frank, Aunt Gert and my mother to the movies. You couldn't skip a week, or you would miss out on your bonus. Bonuses were a pot, dish, glass, or cup handed out as freebies. As a result, our homes all sported the same household utensils. I don't remember the names of the movies she saw. The week before she died, Mother went to the movies. She laughed so loud you could hear her all over the theater.

My mother died suddenly at the age of 43 on March 9, 1948. She collapsed on her way to work that morning. The cause of death was high blood pressure, a cerebral hemorrhage. When Mother died I became head of the family, but my brother Howard ("Hash") worked to support us.

FATHER

My father, Howard Clayton Henry, was born in Sandy Ground and lived with his family at 548 Bloomingdale Road. Like all of us, he was short and bowlegged. He delivered ice and coal for John Gibbs in Perth Amboy, N.J. He would leave the house early in the morning and drive his old Ford onto the ferry at Tottenville.

Most importantly, my father was a musician. He was the leader of "Hash Henry and His High Steppers," a dance band. Mother played the piano in the band. Mr. Charlie Logan was on drums, Hayward Bevans on tenor saxophone, George Smith "Mr. Smitty" (my husband Glemby's stepfather) sometimes played the saxophone, and Vanig Houesepian (Turk van Lake was his stage name), from Annadale, played the guitar. My father played the saxophone, the clarinet and sometimes the drums.

My earliest memory of Father was his practicing the saxophone in our home at 569 rear Bloomingdale Road. We children were made to practice singing regularly and learned every song. One of the songs I remember is "Pennies from Heaven." Father's band performed at Asbury Park nightclubs. I was never permitted to attend his performances.

My father was not home much, but he laid down the law, via my mother. The cat-o'-nine-tails hung in the basement. As I look back upon my childhood I really question whether all of his rules were for our benefit or his. His papa was a severely strict man, so that's the way he treated us.

Although at that time my father did not go to church on Sundays, we were

Howard Clayton Henry, ca. 1921. *This photograph of Lois Mosley's father may have been taken just prior to his marriage to Susan Ann Landin. Howard was always a smart dresser. (Unless otherwise stated, all family photographs are from the collection of Lois Mosley.)*

not allowed to run, jump or play as we did during the week. It was church, church, church and sit on the porch. The only deviation from that rule was that we were allowed to go down Bloomingdale Road to Reinhardt's ball field to watch my daddy play ball. Sometimes on Sunday, we jumped into the rumble seat of his Model T Ford and went for a ride. If there was a flat tire we children fixed it.

My papa was a rolling stone. It took many years after his death to learn how far he rolled. My mother must have been an extraordinary and forgiving woman to have protected my father as she did. Mother lived with her problems, but never did she say a word to her children

The Eagle Athletic Club on the field at Reinhardt's, ca. 1927. *Howard Clayton Henry, Lois's father, is seated at the right end of the middle row. He was a pitcher and sometimes catcher. Seated next to Howard is Fred Roach, who became a well-known taxi driver. In 1934 a reporter described "Hash" Henry as "the grand old man of baseball." While playing with the Sandy Ground Pirates against the Pleasant Plains Athletic Club, he was "up to his customary perfect form and was all over the field, playing fautless ball."* Staten Island Transcript, *May 17, 1933, p. 1, col. 2.*

about or against our father. Even though he did get his life straightened out some time after my mother's death, he was a troubled man. There were things he wanted to tell me about his indiscretions. He'd start to and then renege. He didn't have the courage to face the truth.

My father was not alone with his indiscretions in Sandy Ground. Very few people in Sandy Ground could afford to throw stones. But I am happy that we know and understand this side of our family's history. We are a united family; we are concerned about each other and love each other very much.

Original Dixieland Ramblers, ca. 1930. *"Hash" Henry is on the far right. When his band played at the Tottenville Casino in July 1934, it was called "Hash Henry's Dixie Syncopators." A reporter related, "Several hundred additional young people were attracted to the Tottenville Beach on Wed. evening by the strains of Hash Henry's Dixie Syncopators playing at Larry Bredbeck's five-cents-a-dance palace at the Tottenville Casino. The Park plan inaugurated there recently has become increasingly popular. Over seven hundred dancers can dance on the floor at one time." Staten Island Transcript, July 22, 1934, p. 3, col. 3.*

Five other children are attributed to my father. Four are the children of Gladys Moody, who lived first on Clay Pit Road and later on Bloomingdale Road. They are Dora, Donald, Harold and Howard Moody. Edna Henman, who lived at 704 Bloomingdale Road, was the mother of Clayton Henman. I would have loved knowing that Clayton Henman was my half-brother. We always had fun together, sometimes in a painful way. He would twist my arm or call me names, but giggle like crazy when it was over. When he became a city bus driver in Brooklyn, I happened to get on his bus one day and he called out to me, "Hey farmer, from the country!" You can be sure that I avoided his bus after that.

My father spent his last years dedicating himself to the Rossville A.M.E. Zion Church. He tried his best to make restitution for his mistakes. May he rest in peace.

Howard Clayton Henry, ca. 1976. *Lois's father playing the saxophone on Family Day at the Rossville A. M. E. Zion Church. In 1939 Howard separated from his Sandy Ground family and lived in New Jersey. He was for many years a crane operator at Koppers Inc., in Carteret. Divorced from Lois's mother, he married Virginia Jeffers and lived in Long Branch, N.J., until his death in 1979. In his retirement years he returned to Sandy Ground nearly every weekend to participate in church activities.*

GRANDFATHER AND GRANDMOTHER HENRY,
THEIR ANCESTORS AND THEIR CHILDREN

My father's parents were Francis Matthias Henry and Mary Emily Landin. They were married in Sandy Ground on Jan. 20, 1886, and lived at 548 Bloomingdale Road. I have their marriage certificate. Francis was born on Staten Island. He became an oysterman who owned the sloop *Fanny Fern*.

His father, John Jackson Henry, was also born on Staten Island. John Jackson Henry was one of the founders of the Rossville A.M.E. Zion Church, in 1850. According to a family tradition, John Jackson Henry purchased two and one-half acres in Sandy Ground from Isaac Winant in 1870.

John Jackson Henry's father, whose first name we do not yet know, is believed to be the first generation of our family to have settled on Staten Island. A freed slave, he came here from elsewhere in New York State. His wife was Frances Jackson Henry, a sister of Capt. John Jackson.

Mary Emily Landin Henry, my grandmother, was also from a second-generation Sandy Ground family. The Henrys and the Landins were highly respected on Staten Island by both white and black residents.

Francis and Mary Emily had eight children: Everett, Fred, Edith, Lillian, Flora, Helen, Howard (my father) and Evelyn.

My aunts and uncles were an important part of my childhood. They were a very talented family and grew up to follow careers in education, music and art. They became an example to me and to all the people of Sandy Ground.

Everett taught grammar school and was an assistant principal in Egbertville and later at P.S. 12 in Concord. His face being black kept him from the title of principal even though he did the work. He had an M.A. in English from New York University. He and his wife Edna lived at 399 Davis Avenue, Livingston. He was a very proper speaker. We children had to be careful of our sentence structure when talking to Uncle Everett. He was very active in the Staten Island community, becoming president of the local chapter of the NAACP.

Fred was an auto mechanic who owned a garage in Perth Amboy, N.J. He invented a heater for automobiles, but according to him Henry Ford stole his invention and patented it.

Edith was a great homemaker who raised her sister Evelyn and her brother Howard when their mother passed. She was a beautician.

Lillian was a singer who was trained by a professor in New York City. I had the honor to accompany her at recitals at our church. A graduate of Pratt Institute, she majored in costume design.

Flora recited Negro poetry in dialect on special occasions at the A.M.E. Zion Church. "Asleep at the Switch" and "Little Brown Baby" were her favorites. (For more about Aunt Flora, see p. 94.)

Helen lived in Sandy Ground all her life and never married. She taught us children respect for our elders. As an older person she went to Tottenville Trade School in the evening. She was a volunteer for S.E.R.V.E. (Serve and Enrich Retirement with Volunteer Experience) for 12 years. (For more about Aunt Helen, see p. 96.)

Howard, my father, was an excellent musician and ballplayer.

Evelyn was a schoolteacher licensed to teach in Perth Amboy, N.J. She lived there with her husband Louis and her sister Edith. She was later an administrator of social services with the NYC Board of Education.

A ninth child, Roy, was Francis Henry's son by his second wife, Mamie Bishop. Roy served in the U.S. Army and worked in a bank on Wall Street.

TOP LEFT: Edith Henry, ca. 1910. *Edith, Lois's aunt, married John Gibbs of Perth Amboy and raised a large family. She was a beautician and a great homemaker.*

TOP RIGHT: Edith Henry Gibbs, ca. 1950.

LEFT: Josephine Henry (left) and Lillian Augusta Henry, ca. 1905. *Aunt Jo was a sister of Francis M. Henry, Lois's paternal grandfather. She lived on the top floor at 548 Bloomingdale Road. Later in life she moved to Asbury Park, N.J., to live with her son. Aunt Jo lived to be 101 years old. Lillian was a daughter of Francis M. Henry and Mary Emily Henry.*

TOP LEFT: Evelyn Henry, ca. 1930. *An accomplished singer of religious and operatic works, Aunt Evelyn studied with Alexander Gatewood in Manhattan and performed in many concert halls and churches. She was brought up in Perth Amboy and taught school there. Her husband was Louis Pennyfeather. Later she was an administrator of social services with the NYC Board of Education and a Brooklyn resident.*

ABOVE: Lillian Henry and Helen Henry, ca. 1950.

TOP RIGHT: Lillian Augusta Henry, ca. 1910. *Aunt Lillian studied voice in Manhattan and sang beautifully. She was a graduate of the Pratt Institute.*

THE LANDINS AND THEIR CHILDREN

My Landin great-grandfathers were the first in our family to come to Staten Island from Maryland. My paternal great-grandfather was Robert Landin. His brother, Dawson Landin Sr., was my maternal great-grandfather.

Dawson Landin Jr., Mother's father, was an oysterman and farmer who had eight brothers and sisters. He and his father, Dawson Landin Sr., owned a 40-foot sloop named the *Pacific*. Robert Landin owned the 30-foot sloop *Independence*.

When my grandpa's oystering and clam-digging days ended, he and other Sandy Grounders turned to the soil and sold their crops. Strawberries, sweet potatoes, melons and tomatoes were some of the principal ones. I was too young to remember Grandpa "Dorse." He died long before I was born, but I know he was a supporter of the Rossville A.M.E. Zion Church.

There were many tales of the reasons why they were put out of the oystering business. It was said the beds were polluted. Competition with the whites caused many problems.

Grandma Landin (Georgiana Harris), wife of Dawson Landin Jr., was a gracious, quiet lady with snow-white hair. She was born in Staten Island and she and Grandpa were married in the A.M.E. Zion Church in Sandy Ground in 1863. They lived at 187 Sharrott's Road, which had been my great-grandfather Landin's home, too. They had four children: Gertrude, Frances, Susan (my mother) and Kenneth.

Grandma loved to can fruits and vegetables and make preserves. You never tasted apple butter until you tasted Grandma's. Grandma also made apple cider and root beer. That was the best! Aunt Gertrude, her daughter, who never married, lived and slept with Grandma upstairs in the big room with the feather bed.

Georgiana Harris Landin (Mrs. Dawson Landin Jr.), ca. 1930. *Lois's maternal grandmother lived at 187 Sharrott's Road. Her husband was Dawson Landin Jr., an oysterman.*

If you have slept in a feather bed you will know what I experienced. It's terribly uncomfortable. All the occupants roll toward the middle! Even so, my cousin Lenora Moore, Aunt Frances's daughter, and I always wanted to spend the weekends at Grandma's house. We were gluttons for punishment. We had to sleep between the two ladies and not move a muscle all night long. Every time you breathed hard and moved, they would threaten us and say, "Lay still child!" However, we never quit asking to sleep over.

Aunt Gert was the community piano teacher. We were taught to read music and play the scales. It was very important to keep your wrists up while playing the piano. Every time you let your fingers down they would get cracked by Aunt Gert's pencil. She had been taught the piano by Mrs. Wilbur, a white woman, who lived in Pleasant Plains. Aunt Gert was also a seamstress.

During my childhood Kenneth Dawson Landin ("Uncle Kenny" or "Uncle Dorsey"), Grandma Georgiana's son, lived with his mother and Aunt Gert. When he was old enough he became the breadwinner of the family. He was a good uncle and Mother used him to help raise the children. He was our chaperon whenever we went out.

When Uncle Kenny worked for the Works Progress Administration he would give ten cents to each family of his two sisters' children, the

LEFT: Gertrude Landin (Aunt Gert), *top left*; Walter McCoy; Flora Henry (Aunt Flossie), *bottom left*; Lillian Augusta Henry, ca. 1920. *Walt McCoy was a family friend who lived at 599 Bloomingdale Road. He later moved to Brooklyn.*

RIGHT: Gordon Landin, Eighth Grade Graduation, P.S. 3, ca. 1930. *Gordon was the son of William Landin and Ella Bishop Landin. He died at Richmond Memorial Hospital on Dec. 3, 1934, at age 16, while undergoing a tonsillectomy. As recorded in the* Staten Island Transcript *of Dec. 8: "The A.M.E. Zion Church was filled and many persons had to stand at the funeral. .... A set of resolutions from the Sabbath School was read by Superintendent John H. Henman, and from Boy Scout Troop No. 50 by Harrison Ethridge, Jr. The choir sang Gordon's favorite hymn, "Peal Out the Watchword," also "Lead Kindly Light," "Abide with Me," "Shall We Meet Across the River?" and "Safe in the Arms of Jesus."*

Moores and the Henrys. Since there were four children in each family, one of the four children in each family took turns getting the two extra cents on Fridays. It was tough waiting for Uncle Kenny to come to our house on payday. Of course the money burned a hole in our pockets. We could hardly wait to go to Stout's or Reinhardt's to buy our penny's worth of candy.

Uncle Kenny also gave us children our weekly bath in the old tin tub. We didn't know that it was unsanitary to take a bath in someone else's water. When that Octagon soap got on you, or the soap that Mother made in the backyard with lye, you were clean! Mum was the deodorant of the day.

Childhood Memories

When the Henry children lived at 548 Bloomingdale Road, we were in bed by 7:00 P.M. every night. We slept upstairs. Many nights, especially in the summer, we would peek out the upstairs windows and watch the neighborhood children at play.

Fun

From October to February or March we went sleighriding and ice skating. We slid down Bloomingdale Road and skated on the pond behind 548 Bloomingdale Road. Sometimes our sled was an old cardboard box acquired from the grocery store. Other times we were lucky if the Salvation Army managed to give us a second-hand sleigh for Christmas. A new one was usually something to hope for.

In the summer, orange crate cars built by the boys of Sandy Ground were a source of much entertainment. A piece of rope fastened to the front wheels was used to steer. The boys might even acquire a license plate and made their cart something else! Many unsuspecting persons lost their skate wheels to these go-carts. There were some fierce races.

Bruises and many a skinned knee were the results of go-cart mishaps. We had some good times racing one another down Woodrow and Bloomingdale Roads. It's wonderful now to remember all the fun we had 70 years ago.

We also played kick the can, marbles, mumblety-peg, hide and seek, pussy in the corner, dodge ball, and stick ball. Every once in a while, we had relay races. Everybody had a penknife or an ice pick that we used to play toe-knee-chest-nut and other games. Imagine how low-key we were, a knife or ice pick was never thought of as a weapon by us children.

Mary Emily, my sister, reminds me of the time we were playing follow the leader. We lived at 570 Bloomingdale Road, the two-family house to the left of the church. Lenora, my Landin cousin, was the leader and she decided that we should jump up on the porch with two feet. Well, Mary Emily didn't quite make it. She cut her leg to the white of the bone and had to be taken to Richmond Memorial Hospital for stitches. Once healed, she had to go back and have the stiches removed. We made her walk to Prince's Bay to save the nickel bus fare.

We walked many miles when we were growing up. It was no big deal for the bunch of us to walk to Prince's Bay Beach or Wolfe's Pond to go swimming. I don't believe it hurt any of us. Our parents had it much harder. Cars were scarce in our families. If there was a car the father usually took it to work. You could be pretty popular if you had a car and could share the rumble seat with your friends.

WALKING THROUGH HOLLOW PASS

Hollow Pass was on the way to Pleasant Plains, where we often walked on business for our parents. Our greatest threat was walking through Hollow Pass on Bloomingdale Road, beyond Ike Harris's house. Walking alone or with a scaredy-cat like me was a great feat. We would have to maneuver past Hauber's cows on Bloomingdale Road in Pleasant Plains

The Henry sisters with Lorraine Gibbs, ca. 1948. *Seated on the piano bench at 569 Bloomingdale Road. Left to right: Lois, Lorraine, Mary Emily and Frances. Lorraine, the Henry sisters' cousin, is a daughter of John Gibbs and Edith Henry Gibbs, Lois's aunt.*

Heights. They almost always seemed to be grazing on both sides of the road. The trick was to walk between the cows and reach your destination. I was afraid that "Wandering Buster," a man who lived in the Hollow, might catch me. Sometimes our strict teacher, Mrs. Flora McVay, and her sterner sister, Lucy Roberts, would make us stay after school and miss the bus home. That meant that we had to walk home alone without a friend.

REINHARDT'S

Reinhardt's, located at the southwest corner of Bloomingdale Road and Sharrott's Road, was a combination ice cream, candy store and saloon. It was an amusement park for white folks and it provided much fun for us Sandy Ground kids. They had a ball field supervised by Mr. Charlie Bucks. Busloads of people would invade Sandy Ground for the mammoth picnics that were held at Reinhardt's. It was also named "The Neighbor" and in 1972 its name was changed to "Sleepy Hollow Inn."

The bold kids, mostly the boys, would go down to Reinhardt's and entertain the picnic folks. They would show off and dance and the people would give them nickels. Sometimes the bolder kids would steal the little red reflectors from the license plates on the patrons' cars. At these picnics and clambakes, the picnickers ate and drank all day long. When evening came we kids became beggars. We would run home and get our pots and pans and the people would give us the leftover food and clam chowder to take home.

We were usually a quiet neighborhood but I do remember the fight

LEFT TO RIGHT: Mary Emily Henry, Lois's sister; Helen Henry, Lois's aunt; and Frances Henry, Lois's sister, ca. 1940.

Sandy Ground boys pose for the camera, ca. 1926. Left to right: *Clifford Henry, Aunt Helen Henry's son; Gordon Landin, son of William Landin (Uncle Billy); Hayward Bevans, son of Aunt Beatrice Landin Bevans; Kenneth Landin (Uncle Kenny), son of Dawson Landin Jr.*

that erupted in 1935 between a few Sandy Ground men and some of the patrons at Reinhardt's. A paddy wagon took John Cooper, Lester Moody ("Leaky") and others to jail.

SCHOOL

I attended P.S. 31 in Sandy Ground, as did my brothers and sisters and my mother before us. Mrs. Hurd was my first teacher. Ours was a two-room school, but we only used one room. There were only three grades, first, second and third, and all were in one room, with just one teacher. We had a six-month curriculum. There was a progression from 1A to 1B, 2A to 2B, 3A to 3B. So if you happened to get left back, you would only be a few months behind in your grade. In those days we sang a song and read Scripture each day. We saluted the flag, recited the pledge of allegiance and sang "America." There were only a few white kids at P.S. 31. We thought of it as the Sandy Ground school.

Later Miss Kreischer, who married and became Mrs. Sleight, was our teacher. She was my favorite teacher. She was impressed with Walter (Buddy) McDonald and me and we both skipped a grade, which made us a bit younger than the other kids.

After graduation from P.S. 31 we were bused to P.S. 3 in Pleasant

Plains. At P.S. 3 Negro children were a minority. Some teachers were insensitive to the kids from Sandy Ground, but the Hillard sisters and Mrs. Seguine were three who were fair to all their students. Mrs. Flora McVay and Mrs. Lucy Roberts, who were sisters, seemed very prejudiced. We even put down our race because we were made to feel ashamed of our blackness. Any time the word "black" or a similar expression was made, we had to repeat the words or read aloud out of the book. We sang "Old Black Joe," "Swanee River," and "My Old Kentucky Home" as if they were the only songs the teacher knew. Never in my early schooling was I ever told that black persons made contributions to our culture. Even today, little is taught about black history. We must look to our church and to black organizations to glean just what we are all about.

If there was a peculiar smell in the room, Mrs. Roberts would go up and down the aisle sniffing. She always stopped at a black child's seat. Then she would embarrass you whether or not the odor came from you. I was such a skinny child that she often made an example of me by asking what I had for breakfast and checking up on what I ate for lunch. I had to count how many times I chewed my food so that I did not upset my digestion. Sometimes we hid food in our clothes and threw it away later. My days at P.S. 3 were not my happiest.

We felt so sad when the city closed P.S. 31. It was a mad scramble to see who could make the most from the "junk." The inkwells were made of brass. Desks and other furniture were stolen. All of our parents had graduated from P.S. 31, so there was a strong relationship between it and Sandy Ground families.

When P.S. 31 closed, the kids were divided into three districts. Some went to P.S. 6 in Rossville. Others went to P.S. 3 in Pleasant Plains. The remainder went to P.S. 4 in Kreischerville.

When I was in grammar school, it was discovered that I had a leaky heart. I am sure that my physical problems today did not start at age 50,

Frances Henry, *right,* and Yvonne Usry, on Graduation Day from Tottenville High School, 1950. *They are standing in front of 575 Bloomingdale Road. Frances is Lois's sister. Yvonne is a daughter of William and Vera Usry and a granddaughter of Robert H. Landin and Rebecca Gray Landin. Yvonne married Elmore R. Taylor in 1959. A retired NYC schoolteacher, Mrs. Taylor continues to live on Staten Island today and is a leader in the Rossville A.M.E. Zion Church. She was the founding president of the Sandy Ground Historical Society and a 1984* Staten Island Advance *Woman of Achievement.*

May Day, P.S. 3, Pleasant Plains, ca. 1935. *Lois is standing front row center. In the second row, second from the left, is Wendell Etheridge; second from the right, Walter ("Buddy") McDonald. Miss Lynn, Principal, in the dark hat, is standing back row center.*

Eighth Grade Graduation, P.S. 3, Pleasant Plains, 1940. *Lois Henry standing far left. Walter ("Buddy") McDonald, far right, second row. Eleanor Donaghy, Lois's best friend at P.S. 3, seated far left. The girls all made their own dresses. Center front row: Miss Lynn, Principal* (left) *and Mrs. Flora McVay, teacher.*

but were lying dormant for many years. My mother used to take me to Bellevue Clinic in New York City for treatment. I don't recall taking any medication, but my physical activities had to be limited. I was not allowed to run, hop, or skip with the other children at school. I was always the scorekeeper or some other non-physical sports participant.

After graduating from the eighth grade we all went to Tottenville High School. It was not until I went to high school that they decided I was physically all right.

I was then allowed to participate in all physical education activities. Being skinny worked to my advantage. I was a very fast runner. I had a lot of stored-up energy. I enjoyed volleyball, basketball, and especially softball. In basketball, I was a guard. We played "girls' style" in those days. You stayed on your half of the court, bounce and pass, no drib-

LEFT: Lois Henry's graduation photograph, Tottenville High School, 1944. RIGHT: Sleighriding on Bloomingdale Road, 1946. *The Henry sisters: Lois (in hat), Frances (rear), Mary Emily (middle), and little Amorie Louise Bevans, daughter of Hayward and Louise Bevans, on sled. The house on the right is 599 Bloomingdale Road.*

bling allowed. I had a rather strong arm and I loved to stand at one end of the court and sail the ball to my forward at the other end. I also played touch-tackle with the local boys.

Softball, however, turned out to be my major sport. I was a tomboy through and through. When I was high-school age I was the youngest on the local softball team that played regularly at Reinhardt's. Those were good times.

GANGS

When they were growing up the girls could not go to dances without the older guys as escorts. Although there were gangs, they didn't carry knives or guns as they do today. Their weapons consisted of sticks and stones. Each community had its share of young men who tended to overprotect the girls. The boys from Stapleton, Port Richmond or West New Brighton used to travel to the "country" (Sandy Ground) to visit the girls. Sometimes they had to leave in a hurry: The boys of Sandy Ground would chase them away. The boys from Perth Amboy used to be sent home by the boys of Sandy Ground also.

THE ROSSVILLE A.M.E. ZION CHURCH

Everything interesting or entertaining happened at the church. Mr. John Henman was Sunday School Superintendent for many years. Every Sunday we had to sing "Nearer My God To Thee." My little sister Frances had to sing "Yes, Jesus Loves Me." Sunday and church were the normal way of living for Sandy Ground.

In the winter we worshiped in the church basement. This was to save money on fuel. We had good times down there. There was shouting, hallelujahs, amens. Aunt Ethel Harris would get the Holy Spirit and almost fall on the potbelly stove. For us children, it made going to church worthwhile. The love feast that we shared (bread and water) on the fourth Sunday of each month was to prepare us for Communion on the first Sunday of the coming month.

Florence Henman was a hydrocephalic who really enjoyed coming to church. She was a very large girl. Her father, Mr. Gilbert (Tobe) Henman, had to struggle to bring her down the basement stairs in her wheelchair. Florence's disability caused her head to roll from side to side. We all loved her. She was so happy in church. You could hear her singing above everyone with her exciting and joyful voice.

I have been lifelong member of the church and remain active in its many organizations. Despite my limited ability I have played the piano and organ since I was 13. Mother accompanied the Senior Choir and my cousin Frances Harris, Charles Harris's daughter, played for the Junior Choir until she married and moved away. When Mother died in 1948,

I took over and played the organ for the Senior Choir. With little training, I was scared to death, but I managed.

I love my church, but at times I get discouraged at "the powers that
be" who rule the church. We have been treated as a stepchild for as long
as I can remember. They take us for a bunch of backwoods farmers, except when it comes to assessments. I am tired of ministers saying why
the bishop sent them to Rossville to straighten out our problems. Don't
they know they are the problem? We change ministers as we change
clothes.

I remember many of the pastors. The Rev. Amos P. Jenkins and his
family lived at the parsonage at 640 Bloomingdale Road. The Rev. Jenkins
had a son named Sydney who was ring bearer at Mable Decker Munro's
wedding. My sister Mary Emily was flower girl. The Rev. Robert Frazier,
"Peg Leg," as we called him, was a rascal. He had curly hair and looked
like a con man with his peg leg. He used us children to run around town
and sell his trinkets, key rings and such. All the money went to him, but
he would give the kids a small gift. The Rev. and Mrs. P. B. Simmons also
lived in the parsonage. He had a twitchy eye and changed the choir loft
in the church because he didn't want anyone sitting higher up than he
did. We have had some other "lulus." The Rev. William E. Murphy made
many trips to Reinhardt's. The Rev. Moss kept his beverage under the
seat of his car. We have had so many pastors at Rossville, it would re-
quire another book to describe them.

When the Rev. John B. Kirby was pastor (1939-1945), we played
bingo in the church basement. They were hard times. If you were lucky
you might win five pounds of sugar. If you were extra lucky, you would
win a piece of meat. Most of the goodies (canned goods, etc.) were donated by church members. Our church must have had some liberal members because we would have square dancing and a variety of games in
the church basement as our entertainment.

Mr. Chambers was the friendly undertaker. Although he didn't live in Sandy Ground, he buried just about every dead body in town. Whenever he was available, Mr. Chambers would volunteer to help transport our Junior Choir to places where we had to sing. I always remember the thrill of getting into the undertaker's limousine. We didn't choose to ride with Mr. Tobe or "Pop" Pedro; we wanted to ride in the fancy car of Mr. Chambers. At that time we often visited the Rev. Frazier, our former pastor, who had become pastor at Wallace Temple in Bayonne, N.J.

My mother, Susie, was the parent who took charge of our very famous Drum and Bugle Corps. We were partly sponsored by the George Washington Carver Social Club. I was the worst musician in the drum corps. We would lose points because the girl playing the bugle wasn't playing. My brother Hash was really good on the trumpet. Hashie enjoyed music. Billy Grady and Charlie Logan were in competition on the drums. Dotty Harris was our drum majorette.

Three white men, Mr. Woglom, who lived on Sharrott's Road; Mr. Harris, from West Brighton; and Mr. Fred Muche were very generous with their time and patience. They faithfully trained our group without any compensation. Mr. Muche had a sports store on Castleton Avenue. He donated a good portion of the equipment or sold it to us at a reasonable price. The P.A.L. in Tottenville donated our green and white uniforms. You couldn't tell us little folks that we weren't sharp! We often came in second or third in competition.

Ellen Bernice Pedro ("Bern") took over for her father "Pop" Pedro as church sexton when he fell and broke his hip. She also cleaned the church, ran errands and helped to care for many needy persons. Because Bern had suffered from rickets as a child, her height was less than average. Bern's sister Thelma (Nan) was our "measuring tape." When we grew taller and finally passed Nan's height, we were proud. Good-natured Nan never got mad at us kids. I think of Bern as the Cinderella of Sandy Ground. Without complaining she faithfully continued her daily work schedule and never complained until she died at age 78.

I really don't know how I did it, but I also volunteered to play the piano for the Mount Calvary Holiness Chruch on Richmond Terrrace in Port Richmond for their special occasions. In the dead of winter I would walk up from the train station in Pleasant Plains by myself in the evening to get home. Sometimes Gladys Bowers (later Barrigher), who lived at 624 Bloomingdale Road, and I took the bus home together. (Gladys was the stepdaughter of my Uncle Charlie Harris, whose wife was Ethel Mangin Harris.) She had invited me to play for her church. Elder Bass was the pastor. They had no one in the church who could read music. Gladys was the mother of Julius Bowers. "Juli" was godfather to my oldest daughter, Glenda Beth.

T L C

If you hit your children today or threaten them, it's called child abuse. When we were growing up our parents were very liberal. You had to go outside and get your own switch. If the switch broke while you were being waled, you had to go outside and get another. These beatings were usually applied on our bare behinds. Cry and don't cry. If you don't cry you were beat for that. If you cried, you were told to shut up. You wouldn't even think of putting a hand on your bottom to help soften the blows. Child, you were in trouble. You had to learn how to take a beating. There were warnings all day.

"Just wait till your daddy gets home. Still sobbing, huh?"

"No Maw, I'll be quiet."

It took me several hours before I stopped sobbing. If no one took the blame for mischief, all butts lay face up, bare on the bed, and all were punished alike.

Now I ask you: Was that child abuse? No ma'am, just tender loving care. It was a huge lesson in respect. We knew that if our parents only called our name or looked at us hard one time, we had better change our ways. They seldom had to yell at us because we respected their authority.

Sandy Ground mothers also had a very strict rules about our language. Cursing was not allowed. Words I hear young people say today, and also said by some of their parents, would surely never have been allowed. If we so much as said the word "lie," or called someone a liar, we were in big trouble. We never even thought of taking the Lord's name in vain.

The punishment for saying a bad word was announced by, "Get the Octagon soap." Octagon soap had many uses. Mother would have you stick out your tongue, take that awful yellow soap and wash the bad words right out of your mouth. I do believe they were washed out of your mind, too. Not bragging, but I'm glad I didn't have to go through that too often. My brother "Hash" had top honors in that department.

THE COAL STOVE

Everyone in Sandy Ground had a coal stove. In the evening before going to bed the mother of the house would bank the stove. Banking was mastered by most of the people in the house. Pea coal was usually used because it was a small cut of anthracite. Some folks used nut coal. The coal was heaped on the flame and placed in such a manner that the fire received as little oxygen as possible. In the morning our mother would stoke the coals and before long a nice fire would be there to warm the house.

By the side of the stove was the scuttle that held the coal. Coal was stored in a coal bin behind the house. Filling the scuttle was the job of the boys in the house. The girls' job was to get the kindling used to restart the fire if it had gone out. The poker was used to stir the fire. Sometimes if our fire went out we would go to a neighbor's and borrow a shovel of burning coals to start our fire at home. The kids' job also was to separate the cinders from the ash. The ash was used as fertilizer in our garden. Our cinders were used to help the cars get traction in the snow and were also reused in the stove.

William "Pop" Pedro, Charlie Harris, Harold "Buster" Moody, Mr. Mitchell and Hash Henry (my father) were some of the Sandy Ground men who delivered coal. Those coal bags were heavy and the men carried them on their backs. Each bag must have weighed one hundred pounds or more. They were made of sturdy canvas. Pop Pedro worked for many years delivering coal for the Seguines and Rosellis.

THE ICEBOX AND THE REFRIGERATOR

Before we had a refrigerator we had an icebox. Mr. Dan Mitchell, who lived at 191 Sharrott's Road with his wife Malvina, was our iceman. All iceboxes had a water pan underneath to catch the drips. Our parents would buy a 10- or 15-cent piece of ice from Mr. Mitchell. We kids would hang around the truck to grab the chips that fell from the ice as he chipped it. If Mother had enough money, we would get a 25-cent piece of ice and she would make ices or ice cream. Most families also had a box built outside the kitchen window. This would hold our perishable food in cold weather.

When Mother finally managed to buy a Kelvinator refrigerator, we kept it in the living room covered with a quilt, so that the welfare inspectors' people would not take away our relief for having such an extravagance.

THE OUTHOUSE

Some Sandy Grounders and former Sandy Grounders have forgotten their roots and where they come from. Few can deny knowledge of the old outhouses, no matter how high-style you try to be. Some toilets had a door, a window or even a toilet seat, but they all smelled the same.

Our neighbor, Mr. Hunter, had an inside toilet and so did 591 and 599 Bloomingdale Road and 26 Clay Pit Road. I don't remember anyone else being so well off.

PEDDLER MEN

Do you hear those bells outside? It's the ragman coming down the street. We would run into the house and tell our mother. The ragman had an open truck with a scale. He would weigh our rags and give us a small amount of money. Where did all those rags come from? The fish man came every Friday. Mother would buy 50 or 75 cents' worth of fish. We really lived by bells. Once a month the knife and scissor man came to town to sharpen our tools.

THE TELEPHONE

When I was about six years old and we were living at 569 Bloomingdale Road, our mother went on welfare. Welfare allowed her to have a telephone because she was ill. Before we were permitted to have a telephone, the welfare investigators would pop into our house unannounced at any time.

Before we had a real telephone we invented a telephone system of our very own. Between the McDonalds (at 569), the Moores (at 565), and the Henrys (at 569 rear), we had a "Knock, knock" system that was unique. When we had running water installed in the three houses they were all on the same meter. We could turn the faucet off sharply and it knocked. To call a neighbor we each had our code. The number of knocks let you know who should stick their head out the door for a message.

BEDBUGS

Remember the expression, "Quick, Henry, the Flit!"? Or do you prefer to forget? Well, when I was growing up, that was a phrase everyone knew. Today there are insecticides that are more popular: Raid, Black Flag and others. They have less odor so that everyone doesn't know your problem. What am I talking about? Why, the pesky red bugs that interrupted your sleep and made you say, "Ouch!" many a night. Red welts appeared on your skin afterwards.

Red bugs were in fact bedbugs and they used to live in the coils of bedsprings. Old houses were breeding places, but these creatures were found primarly in the bedroom. To get rid of the pests you had to lift off the mattress and light a candle. You could hear the crack of the bugs as each coil was touched. This procedure took place about once every two weeks. Our mattresses had tufts and a button. This would be a breeding place for the bugs. Our parents were very clean about their surroundings. So why we had those bugs, I do not know. Although I have not seen these bugs in many a year, the memory is still fresh.

RELATIVES

AUNT FLOSSIE

Aunt Flossie, my father's sister Flora Henry, was four-foot-plus and fiery. She lived most of her life at 548 Bloomingdale Road. She was very proud of herself and loved to sing in the choir. With her excellent memory she recited Negro poetry in dialect. How happy we little nieces and nephews were to sit around as she dramatized Negro poetry: "Little Brown Baby with Sparkling Eyes" was our favorite. Remember, we didn't have television so we visualized just what the speaker was saying. We did the same thing with radio programs.

Before World War II Aunt Flossie worked as a domestic. During the war she worked at the Raritan Arsenal in Fords, N.J. After the war she moved about. She worked for rich white folks and in fancy hotels, learn-

The Henrys at Thanksgiving, 1947. Beginning lower left: *Aunt Flossie; Aunt Evelyn [partial view]; Louis Pennyfeather; Aunt Helen; Joan Pennyfeather; Mr. Mapp, a family friend; Elsie Gibbs; Clifford Henry, Aunt Helen's son; Lorraine Gibbs; John Gibbs; Amanda Gibbs (John Gibbs's second wife); Arthur Henry; Frederick Henry Jr.; Uncle Fred; Uncle Everett; Lucille Gibbs; Edward Gibbs; Judy Gibbs; Aunt Lillian. At the home of Aunt Evelyn Pennyfeather, 982 Park Place, Brooklyn. Photograph by Burnet Henry.*

ing catering on the job in New York City and Canada.

Aunt Flossie moved Mother and us children out of 548 Bloomingdale Road so that she could start a business there. We moved across the street to 569 rear, one of the baymen's cottages. She used 548 as a small resort, naming it "Chief Staaten Farm." Her clientele came mostly from Manhattan and the Bronx. Umbrellas and lounge chairs were spread out on the front lawn. Croquet was the big activity in the back yard. Aunt Flossie served her guests as if they were celebrities. Many courses made up her gourmet fare. At times she let her 10- and 12-year-old nieces and nephews assist her in serving and taking care of her guests. Sandy Ground never had it so fancy.

She was a woman who believed in saving her money and investing it wisely. We don't know what happened to Aunt Flossie's resources. The fire of 1963 destroyed 548, completely wiping out her business and her will to continue with life. Toward the end of her life she lived with her sister Helen Henry at 591 Bloomingdale Road. Aunt Flossie, when she died, was fighting to keep the LNG tanks out of Rossville and Bloomingdale Road. The LNG tanks had been built to hold liquified natural gas, but community opposition prevented this.

AUNT HELEN

Almost everyone who lived in Sandy Ground remembers Helen Henry, my father's sister. She really tried to better herself. During the Depression she worked for the W.P.A. as an investigator. In the late 1930s she managed to go to night school for three years to learn commercial subjects. During the war she was a lift operator at Pier 6 in Stapleton. She was a transporter and messenger for Bellevue Hospital for many years, making that arduous trip to Manhattan every day. While at Bellevue she made many lifelong friends. She survived many serious illnesses.

Aunt Helen had only one son, Clifford (Kip). She labored all her life to support herself and her son. In later, more prosperous years, she bought 591 Bloomingdale Road from Hayward Bevans. After retirement she was one of the original S.E.R.V.E. (Serve and Enrich Retirement with Volunteer Experience) volunteers at Willowbrook. She was honored many times by them. In 1974 the *Staten Island Advance* named her a Woman of Achievement.

In addition to her son and grandchildren, her greatest pleasure in life was traveling. She was able to enjoy the better things in life that she could not afford in her early struggle to survive.

Aunt Helen was a dickty lady. Proud as she could be. When she lived at 591 she used to sit upon her porch and would speak to everyone who passed. And you had better acknowledge her presence no matter how many times you passed her on that porch. Children who did not speak would find themselves on her not-too-good-a-child list.

My Aunt Helen was a very outspoken member of the Board of Trustees in the church. She worked very hard for the building and cemetery committees. She accumulated many church records which were unfortunately discarded after her death. If Aunt Helen didn't like something, believe me, you knew it. I witnessed many verbal onslaughts at church meetings.

Mr. Oetgen, a white man from Pleasant Plains, was a friend of Aunt Helen. He often came to church with bags full of day-old bread, buns, cake and rolls. He collected them from various bakeries. Sometimes he would bring sneakers or clothing. He was our Good Samaritan.

Today, if you buy your children clothing without brand-name labels, they refuse to wear them. If we had a 25-cent pair of sneakers we felt lucky and shared them with our sisters and brothers. You have heard of the saying, "The first dressed is the best dressed." Well, we lived by that motto.

AUNT FRANK

Everyone called Frances, my mother's sister, Aunt Frank. She and her husband Murphy Moore, who came from Virginia, had four children: Lenora, Lindwood, Beatrice and Calvin. They lived at 565 Bloomingdale Road. My brother and sisters and I and Aunt Frank's and Uncle Murphy's children were raised as one family. Because Aunt Frank had acute asthma, she could never lie down in bed. She sat in a chair or on the chaise lounge. Aunt Frank played the piano and organ for our church. The most vivid recollection that I have of her is how hard she pulled my hair when she combed and braided it. She would say, "Hold still child. I ain't hurting you."

Uncle Murphy was quite a farmer. We children considered it great fun to help him spade the entire backyard and rake it up for planting. We would level the soil and plant the seeds for various vegetables. Murphy Moore loved to trap. The neighborhood boys used to help him empty the traps that he set down in the woods behind 569. He would catch and skin rabbits and possum. Occasionally he would catch a snapping turtle. Those were fun times.

Uncle Murphy was not a teetotaler. He loved to visit Reinhardt's. That was when he treated me the best. When he came back from Reinhardt's he would have a big bottle of soda for me alone. I would sit in front of all the kids and drink it. This did not make me a favorite with my sisters and brother or my cousins. A large bottle of soda in those days cost 15 cents. To top it off, when you returned the bottle you got two cents back, enough to buy some candy.

The Moore family was later struck by a terrible tragedy. Calvin, Aunt Frank and Uncle Murphy's son, drowned on June 17, 1952. The accident happened in Round Pond, one of the Clay Pit ponds, near Rossville, which was used as a swimming hole. He was 24 years old and the father

William Landin ("Uncle Billy"); Hayward Bevans, his grandson; Aunt Beatrice, his daughter; shown in front of 591 Bloomingdale Road in 1941.

of four children. Enrick McDonald, 16 years old, our neighbor at 569 Bloomingdale Road, drowned with him. A third boy managed to save himself.

UNCLE BILLY

William Dawson Landin (Uncle Billy), my grandmother's brother, was very petite and quiet. He was the first black man to work at the S.S. White Dental Manufacturing Co. in Prince's Bay. He lived at 569 Bloomingdale Road. At 6:00 A.M. he left for work. How did he travel? He rode his bicycle. You could set your watch by Uncle Billy. He never wavered from his routine. It took him about half an hour to ride to work and another half hour to come home. If the snow was deep – we did have big snowstorms years ago – and Uncle Billy could not ride his bike, he left home earlier and walked. That was at least a four-mile trip! How many today would be so faithful in our employment habits?

Ella Bishop Landin was Uncle Billy's wife. Their 16-year-old son Gordon died while having a tonsillectomy. Their daughter, Beatrice Ellen

Uncle Billy Landin with his granddaughter Amorie Louise Bevans, ca. 1940. *At 591 Bloomingdale Road. William Landin was the first black man to work at the S.S. White Dental Manufacturing Co.*

Landin Bevans, "Aunt Bea," was as close to me as my own mother. Aunt Bea had one son, Hayward Bevans, who was spoiled by his mother. He acted as if he was my pop.

Uncle Billy had a huge vegetable garden. My cousin Lenora (Lee) Moore (Frances Moore's daughter) and I helped him plant the seedlings and pull weeds. We even helped cultivate the ground. Mrs. Cutting on Sharrott's Road sold him tomato and sweet potato plants. I don't remember what happened to all of the vegetables we harvested, but Aunt Bea did a lot of canning. She was noted for her souse (pork trimmings, chopped and pickled), piccalilli relish, pickles and many other vegetables. Her closet at the bottom of the basement stairs was always neatly lined with her handiwork. It's sad to say none of us ever learned the secrets of preserving from our foremothers.

When Uncle Billy came home on Friday night he signed his check

Hayward Bernard Bevans, graduation photograph, Tottenville High School. *Lois's cousin, son of Gerard Bevans and Beatrice Landin Bevans.*

and gave it to Aunt Bea. She gave it to my cousin Lee and we would walk down to Reinhardt's to cash it. Never in my life did I hear a harsh word from Uncle Billy. He was church treasurer until poor health forced him to resign. He did not linger long. It was always a mystery to me as a child how a person who seemed so healthy could die so quickly.

HAYWARD BEVANS

Hayward Bernard Bevans was the only son of Beatrice Landin Bevans and the grandson of William (Uncle Billy) Landin. They lived at 591 Bloomingdale Road. Hayward's father, Gerard, was a police officer in Manhattan. That was a great thing in those days.

Hayward Bevans and I were raised as big brother and little sister. Although Hayward was only eight years older than I, when he grew up, he thought he was my pop. We children worshiped him as the greatest uncle ever. As a child Hayward was greatly influenced by my father. He dressed like him, imitated him and idolized "Hash" as the greatest. Hayward was taught to play the saxophone by my father. Bold and with lots of self-confidence, he was a ringleader in the crowd that he grew up with.

Hayward was the only Sandy Ground male in his generation to earn a college degree. Most of his friends quit school and went to work to help support their families. After serving in the U.S. Army, Hayward attended New York University and was presented his bachelor's degree on June 11, 1947.

Although born and bred in Sandy Ground, Hayward was a city kid at heart. He became a postman and free-lance accountant. He never forgot the Rossville A.M.E. Zion Church. When he came to visit he would leave an envelope for the church with Mr. Buster Moody and was the most generous contributor on "Family Day," joining the Henry family team to put our family on top. His donation each time of $100 inspired others to increase their gift.

My children looked upon Uncle Hayward as a godfather. They believed he had stock in the national treasury. The word would go around, "Uncle Hayward is here!" Get on line and get your money! Hayward would borrow money if he didn't have it. He died on Oct. 5, 1983. I'm sure his children and grandchildren miss "the godfather" today.

NEIGHBORS

GRANDMA COOPER

Born in 1900, Grandma Cooper was the oldest woman in Sandy Ground for many years. My best memories of the Coopers are those when they were living in the two-family house near Harris Lane. Later they moved into Mrs. Davis's house near the cemetery.

Sadie Roach Cooper ("Grandma" Cooper), Emel Mosley, Elena Mosley, 1987. *"Grandma" Cooper poses with the newly baptized Emel Mosley and her mother Elena (Mrs. Gregory Mosley) in the Rossville A.M.E. Zion Church.*

Grandma Cooper was born Sadie Roach in Sandy Ground. Her parents were the Rev. Louis Roach, a minister of the Rossville A.M.E. Zion Church, and Addie "Grandma" Roach. In 1923 Sadie Roach married John Cooper, a construction worker from Virginia. They had six children: Daisy, Elmer, Melvin, Ralph, Kenneth and Alvin.

Grandma Cooper was an excellent cook. She made the greatest doughnuts and crullers for the neighborhood kids. Her specialities were clam fritters, potato salad, yum-yum cake and cornstarch pudding. Whatever she made would win a blue ribbon at any state fair. At one time Grandma did her best to supplement the family funds by running the Cooper family grocery store at 559 Bloomingdale Road. Only illness forced her to retire.

Grandma attended church right up to the end of her life in 1989. She was a faithful trustee, a member of the missionary society, and a steward. She also sang in the choir. Grandma Cooper was a soft-spoken woman, but she served as a role model for several generations of Sandy Grounders. She did not go out and build great buildings, but she was a person who had enormous influence in the community.

Kenneth Cooper still lives in Sandy Ground. Daisy lives in Georgia and Elmer lives in New Jersey. Melvin and Ralph are deceased, as is Alvin, who died in an auto accident on Richmond Terrace near Snug Harbor.

Daisy, Grandma's oldest daughter, has fond memories of Millie Harris, my second cousin. Millie, with her first paycheck, bought herself, her sister Edith and Daisy each a new dress. All three dresses were alike, except for the color. One was yellow, one pink, and one blue. They were the cat's meow.

Fred Roach, Taxi Driver

Fred Roach, Grandma Cooper's brother, started out in the taxi business as a young man. He eventually owned his own car and had a license to run a taxi stand near the train station in Pleasant Plains. Fred had 71 Clay Pit Road built for his parents, the Rev. Louis Roach and Addie Roach, and lived there also. "Granny Roach," a sweet quiet lady, kept house for Mr. Fred as long as she could.

Initially he found it difficult to obtain a medallion and by the time he finally got one had plenty of competition. Mr. Newton, a white man who lived on Woodrow Road, gave Mr. Fred a hard time. It is alleged that Mr. Newton and another taxi owner plotted against Fred, paying someone to kill him. In fact, Fred Roach was hit upon the head with a club and dumped into the back seat of his car. He managed to crawl to a house on Maguire Avenue to get help. It was never proved who tried to get rid of Fred. The incident frightened his mother. She could not go to sleep un-

Fred Roach, ca. 1950. *Fred Roach was a popular taxi driver, with a taxi stand in Pleasant Plains. He is shown seated outside his home at 71 Clay Pit Road.*

til Mr. Fred came home at night. Sometimes her granddaughter Daisy Cooper stayed with her to keep her company.

The usual cost for a ride in the taxi from Sandy Ground to Pleasant Plains or Prince's Bay was 25¢. Only the affluent could regularly afford such a sweet luxury. The schoolteachers from P.S. 3 liked Mr. Roach. He had a monopoly on their business. He parked his taxi in Pleasant Plains, near the A&P. The storekeeper used to give Mr. Fred stale bread on weekends to take home to his family.

We kids often put one over on Mr. Fred. After lunch at home he would go back to the station in Pleasant Plains. We knew that the way to get a free ride to Pleasant Plains was to start walking about the time we thought he would be passing. We made sure we did not look back to see if he was coming. Most times he would pick us up and give us a free ride.

There was no limit to the number of times our mothers made us walk to the store in Pleasant Plains for groceries or on any other errand. Maybe, if our load was heavy, Mother would give us a quarter for the taxi ride back but we preferred to walk and spend the money for ice cream at Scowcroft's Drug Store. We might even have been lucky enough to have change for candy or a soda at Eisengreen's.

Sometimes when Aunt Bea Bevans and children got out of the taxi returning from Pleasant Plains, we would say, "How much, Fred?" He would reply, "Let me think a moment." Then he'd give us the price. At times there would be more than four people in the taxi, but he never charged the full amount.

Mrs. Jennie Hammond told me she was Fred's first woman driver. The Hammonds were an old Sandy Ground family. She says he trusted her. She drove many years. People would say, "Look out! Here comes Miss Jennie." She would sail pass the light. People felt sorry for her. When her car was stolen, she could not afford to buy a new one. She loved to come to Family Day at church. Later in life she lived in the West Brighton Senior Citizens' complex, where she died.

Mr. Hunter

George H. Hunter and his son William (Willie) had a business building cesspools and cleaning them. We called the truck they used for clean-

ing out cesspools "The Honey Wagon." Mr. Hunter was looked up to as a rather well-to-do man. He lived at 575 Bloomingdale Road. He allowed us to have barn dances down in the garage behind 565-569 Bloomingdale Road. He was the owner's representative for these two houses and 569 rear. After retiring he worked hard for the church, raising money through his barbecues. He was a fabulous cook! He also spent many hours caring for the Rossville A.M.E. Zion Church cemetery.

After the death of his first wife, Celia Ann Finney (1877-1928), daughter of a local oysterman, he married Edith Cook (1877-1938). Both of Mr. Hunter's wives were active in the Rossville A.M.E. Zion Church and community, especially Celia, who used to put on plays and concerts. Everyone wanted to be in Mrs. Hunter's productions. Mr. Daniel Haynes, a friend of Celia's and a professional actor, taught the children the Negro National Anthem, "Lift Every Voice and Sing." He lived in the house of Miss Seguine, our schoolteacher, across from the World War I monu-

LEFT: George Hunter and the "Honey Wagon," ca. 1940. *Written on the truck door is: "Geo. Hunter, Pleasant Plains, S.I., N.Y., Tott-8-1228."*

George Hunter in front of 575 Bloomingdale Road. *Photograph by Therese Mitchell, 1955. Courtesy Staten Island Historical Society. The protagonist of Joseph Mitchell's article, "Mr. Hunter's Grave" (1956). Retired and a widower, George Hunter cooked for Catherine Purnell, his niece, and was very active in the Rossville A.M.E. Zion Church.*

LEFT: William Hunter ("Willie"), ca. 1915. *Son of George and Celia Hunter. His long slender fingers contributed to his talent at playing the piano. "Willie" married and had a son, also named William, who became a NYC police officer.* RIGHT: Willie Hunter and grocer in Pleasant Plains grocery store, ca. 1940. *Most Sandy Grounders shopped in Pleasant Plains.*

ment in Pleasant Plains. Edith Hunter gave ox roasts and barbecues and organized all kinds of games, bringing a good active life to Sandy Ground.

Mr. Willie, Mr. Hunter's son by this first wife, was quite talented at the piano. He would play for us children when he was feeling his cup of tea.

Mr. Hunter Moore, an employee of George Hunter who lived at 522 Bloomingdale Road, met his death while working on the Honey Wagon. It was a horrible death. He fell into a cesspool and drowned. The story of this was published in "Mr. Hunter's Grave," which was written by Joseph Mitchell and appeared in *The New Yorker*, Sept. 22, 1956.

Catherine Purnell, George Hunter's niece, who was orphaned at an early age, was at first raised by Rhodie Purnell, her grandmother. When her grandmother died, Catherine came to live with the Hunters. Edith Hunter was very strict with her and she did not have an easy life while her aunt was alive. Catherine wanted someone to love and she became pregnant at an early age. Having a son, Jimmy Purnell, did not make it any easier for her. While attending school, she only had one close friend, Muriel, who lived on Seguine Avenue in Prince's Bay. Catherine had another love, William Pedro Jr. Bill married a girl from Long Island, a dietitian named Charlotte. Catherine and her son moved to Brooklyn, where she eventually married; her name is now Bland.

UNCLE JIMMY

James Decker ("Uncle Jimmy") lived in a little house at 552 Bloomingdale Road. His house has long been gone.

Twice a year Uncle Jimmy would come to church either an hour early or an hour late, never remembering to reset his clock to or from daylight saving time. Uncle Jimmy was the town barber, but at the pace he moved you had better eat before you entered his house for a haircut. Like Uncle Billy Landin, Uncle Jimmy rode a bicycle. He would fasten his barber supplies on his wheel and away he'd go. Uncle Jimmy loved to

The Rev. James S. Decker (Uncle Jimmy), 1908. *Detail from broadside, p. 175.*

make chocolate layer cakes. I don't know what he put into his chocolate, but I've never been able to find anything like it.

Uncle Jimmy was also our local minister. He married and baptized many Sandy Ground people. The A.M.E. Zion Conference never actually assigned him to a church, but he often substituted for our regularly assigned pastor.

WILLIAM HARRIS

William Harris (who was called "Mr. Wee," for what reason was not clear to me) and his wife Lena lived at 587 Bloomingdale Road. They had purchased the house in the 1920s from John Tyler, an oysterman, who had built it in 1883. The Harrises got all of their water from the well behind their house. Many homes, including ours, got water the same way.

Before coming to Sandy Ground, Mr. Harris lived in Jersey City, where he carried ashes and garbage for a living. After moving to Staten Island, he worked as a flagman and a watchman. He also worked in Manhattan. He lost his eye in an explosion. Lena Harris did housework in Tottenville and its vicinity. They had two daughters: Sabella, born in Jersey City, and Marion, born in Sandy Ground. The girls attended Tottenville High School. Sabella died in 1924 at age of 21. Her mother Lena died at an early age due to a heart condition.

Mr. Harris was one of the first Sandy Grounders to own a car, an old-fashioned one that you cranked to start. He and that old Model-T Ford would go "putt, putt, putt" up and down Bloomingdale Road. Mr. Harris later retired on his pension. I do not know how he survived financially. It seemed to me that he was always an old man.

Marion Harris married William Payne of Jersey City. Their two children, Lena and William Payne Jr. (Billy), came to live with their grandparents at 587 Bloomingdale Road and went to school on Staten Island.

Billy and I share the same birthday. We attended P.S. 3 in Pleasant

Plains together. Billy was a great athlete, excelling in many sports in college. He received a bachelor of science degree from N.Y.U. He now teaches in Jersey City, where he resides with his family.

THE GRADYS

Mr. Dennis Grady and his wife Cora, who lived at 599 Bloomingdale Road, had a large family: Dennis, Julia Belle, Melvin, William, Marie, Peggy, Nancy, Joseph and Jean. Jean was born after they left Sandy Ground. William shared with me his memories of our childhood. Billy and Melvin were among the lucky few who had a bicycle, but they would fight over it and were grounded by their father. They would take turns riding to Pleasant Plains to pick up their food supplies. Like us, they were on welfare.

Billy remembers going over to the Coopers' house adjacent to the Crabtree Avenue cemetery to listen to the radio, which ran on batteries. To us it was a great invention.

MRS. ROBINSON

Mrs. Robinson was born in Georgia in 1847 and lived to be over 100 years old. She was born Adeline Arrington. Her father was a white slave owner who gave her his surname. Family tradition says that Adeline, although born a slave, was allowed to attend school. Her first husband and their son Frank Miles and her second husband, a Mr. Robinson, were born in Valdosta, Georgia. She and Mr. Robinson moved to Perth Amboy, N.J. In 1917 the Robinsons came to Sandy Ground, settling at 605 Bloomingdale Road. Mr. Robinson worked in New Jersey, traveling by a small boat each day. Mrs. Robinson's great-granddaughter, Josephine (Josie), b. 1930, lived at No. 605 and attended P.S. 31.

For us small children No. 605 always seemed spooky. That did not keep us mischievous and nosey kids away. We would sneak over to Mrs.

Robinson's house at night to steal hickory nuts. She would creep out and scare us. In a spooky voice, she would say, "I spies you by yonder land. Get out of here." We kids imagined her as a witch and ran as if the devil was chasing us.

SIS SMITH

Elizabeth Brooks Mosley Smith, my husband's mother, was fondly called "Miss Sis" by everyone. She came from Oyster Bay, Long Island. When she was very young, she married Glemby Mosley of Bayonne, N.J. They had two children, Glemby Jr., my husband, and his sister Thelma. When Miss Sis first came to Sandy Ground, she lived on Cannon Avenue, down the road a piece near the Arthur Kill Road. Cannon Avenue was then a dirt path. It no longer exists. The house was owned by Miss Hattie Robinson.

Miss Sis divorced Glemby and he continued to live in Bayonne. She married George Smith (Mr. Smitty). The Rev. J. B. Kirby performed the ceremony shortly after they moved to 718 Bloomingdale Road. This house had belonged to the Harpers.

Miss Sis was a good dancer. She loved to dance and bump and grind. She had beautiful natural hair and did she love to laugh! When she felt good she would entertain us kids with her whistling. Although my mother used to say, "Whistling women and a crowing hen never came to no good end," I did not relate this rhyme to Miss Sis. We loved her.

My children should know that their grandmother had a heart of pure gold. She was always available to help the sick, whether it was doing the ironing or cleaning the house. She helped me a lot when my mother died in 1948. Miss Sis had many friends, mostly part of the gang from down in the woods. Mrs. Frances Williams and Miss Vivian Smith were two of them. It was a sad day when Miss Sis suddenly died from an apparent bout of indigestion, which was later discovered to have been a heart attack.

Shortly after Miss Sis died, Mr. Smitty, who played in my father's band, married Cora Lytell, Aunt Anna Mae Landin's cousin. They sold the house at 718 and moved to Gordon Street in Stapleton. Mr. Smitty, who was in the junk business, operated a truck out at the dump near Arthur Kill Road in Rossville. Lil Sarjeant lives at No. 718, which she and her husband purchased from Mr. Smitty.

GERALDINE HENMAN MCDONALD

Geraldine, who was born in 1908, lived with her parents, Walter and Alice Henman, at 768 Bloomingdale Road, next to the Potter's Field. The cemetery was owned by the Rossville A.M.E. Zion Church and had been set apart so poor folks could have a decent burial. It was Geraldine's playground. Her favorite tombstone was a long slab that looked like an ironing board. She remembers the following epitaph written on it:

> *Stop and look as you pass by.*
> *For where you are, so once was I.*
> *And where I am you soon will be.*
> *Prepare for Death and follow me.*

Geraldine married Hugh Enrick McDonald, who emigrated from Jamaica. They were the parents of two boys and two girls: Walter, Edna, Gloria and Hugh Enrick (Enny Mac).

Walter Henman's brothers and sisters were Gilbert (Tobe), Lulu, Edward and Henrietta. His father was George Edward Henman. George Edward Henman's father, John Henman, was kidnapped as a child and forced to work as a slave on a ship. He was later able to buy his freedom. When he returned home, his family did not understand him because he spoke only Spanish.

THE BIG SISTERS

Edna and Isabel Vanderhost were sisters who lived at 221 Sharrott's

Road. We called them "The Big Sisters" because they were obese. They kept boarders. I recall a Mr. Oakie (Oklahoma), who had one eye and wore a black patch. Edna married late in life and had no children. Mrs. Isabel was a seamstress. Her son Otis was born in 1913. I never knew who his father was. When Otis grew up, he married Dorothy Sarjeant and they had a daughter known as Dolly. Isabel later married Bill Jones, a shipyard worker in Rossville who died before my time. They were the parents of Robert (Bob) Jones, born in 1916.

During the World War II Bob was a Second Class Seaman, stationed in San Diego, Calif. He married Lelia Griffin, daughter of Harry and Edna Griffin. Before she married Bob, Lelia lived at one of the two pink boarding houses at Woodrow Road and Bloomingdale Road. They had two children, Roberta and Otis. (Information about the Jones family was obtained from my interview with Robert Jones on Sept. 10, 1988, at St. Vincent's Hospital, where he was a patient. He died later that year.)

THE DANIELS—DOWN IN THE WOODS

Theodore and Mae (Willie) Daniels lived on a dirt road "down in the woods" on Norman Street at the end of today's Clay Pit Road. They had eight children: Annie Nubia, Alex Nubia, Teddy, Carmilla, Roger, Charles, Robert and Joyce. Some of the family still live on Staten Island.

Mr. Daniels was a tall, thin man. Mrs. Daniels was a buxom woman. They found many ways to punish one another. He made Mrs. Daniels feed the chicks and chickens. One day, to get even with him, she stepped on all the baby chicks. Another time, when Mr. Daniels went to work, she fixed him good. She put on his one and only suit and of course she burst the seams. While in the suit she cut wood, cooked and did her house chores. When he came home from work she told him she had a surprise for him. She showed him his suit. I wonder who got the surprise after that.

Lois Mosley and Carmilla Daniels, Sept. 1988. *Recovering from surgery, Lois Mosley began writing* Sandy Ground Memories. *Former Sandy Ground resident Carmilla Daniels shared her rollicking memories of "Down in the Woods" with Lois.*

Another time, Mr. Daniels gave Mrs. Mae a $20 bill. This did not satisfy her. She was angry. Mae fed the $20 bill to the pig. When she came to her senses and started thinking that she wanted her $20 back, she fed the pig Ex-Lax. It didn't work. Mrs. Mae killed that pig but the money was never found.

The Daniels made "white lightning" down in the woods. I suppose our parents knew, but it was news to me when I learned that they had a still back there.

Carmilla said that she and her brother Teddy were playing in the woods one day when they came across some glass bottles buried in the ground, covered by wood planks. Carmilla and Teddy broke all the bottles and proudly carried the planks home. They put them behind the shed in their yard. They were so excited they told their father what good children they were and showed him what they had done. Mr. Daniels couldn't believe his eyes or ears. That day Carmilla and Teddy got one of the worst beatings of their lives. They had to climb up into a tree to escape the wrath of their father. Anyway, this story ends later when IRS men went out into the woods searching for the still. They walked over the broken glass but never found what they were looking for.

Carmilla (now married to John Goode) recalls the many animals around their house: pigs, chickens, ducks and a goose. She hated the old goose that used to chase her around the yard and nip her. She eventually rung his neck and buried him. Her papa asked what happened to the goose, but no one knew. Many other animals disappeared in the same manner.

One day Carmilla was walking in the woods and she stepped on what appeared to be a huge rock. The rock moved. She grabbed it by the tail and dragged it home. Her daddy took that big snapping turtle away from her and told her to let it go. Carmilla swears to this day that Mrs. Eastman, a neighbor across the street, made soup out of her turtle.

Carmilla recalls barbecue time when the Daniels would kill a pig and roast it on a spit. Mr. "Skin Tom" was the greatest barbecue man Sandy Ground ever had. Many have tried to imitate Mr. Tom, but they only fool themselves. The aroma from his cooking would surround Sandy Ground. He would get ready to cook on Friday morning. The barbecue started on Friday evening and would end on Sunday. He'd never give you a piece of meat until it was tender and done. It is a pity "Skin Tom" took his secret to the grave for his special sauce.

As a sort of punishment, Teddy and Carmilla had to take the goat to a brown barn in the woods. She says she didn't care even if they didn't get supper, because there were plenty of berries and fruit growing wild. There was also a stream where they could get fresh water. Teddy was so mad he bit the goat.

The Daniels had a boarder named Willie Christan (Mr. Chris). One day he came home full of pride telling Mrs. Mae that he had gotten a promotion on this job and he was going to have lunch with his boss. He asked Mrs. Daniels to make him a special lunch to suit this purpose. Imagine his surprise when he started eating his special lunch and realized he was eating a black-eyed pea sandwich. The peas fell out all over him. Apparently Mr. Chris made Mrs. Daniels mad before she prepared his lunch and his lunch didn't turn out at all the way he expected.

Mrs. Mae also had another boarder named Mr. Jim Doby. He was a short round man with a beer belly. Mr. Doby made daily trips to Reinhardt's saloon. He made it down Bloomingdale Road to Reinhardt's but returning up the hill he was a little wobbly. The kids got a kick out of watching Mr. Doby walking up the road while singing about his Kathleen and quoting Scripture. Sometimes he stumbled and fell but he never hurt anyone.

MR. AND MRS. MANGIN

Next door to the Daniels, also on Norman Street, lived old Mr. Mangin and his wife, who was white. Mrs. Mangin always rode in the back seat of their car. We never knew why. They were not very sociable. The Mangins spent a great deal of time fighting and arguing with the Daniels. Mr. Mangin constantly called the police. During one of these battles, while the police were there, Mrs. Daniels reached over the fence and punched Mr. Mangin. Then she had the nerve to turn around and punch the policeman.

THE EASTMANS AND THE "GOOD TIME CROWD"

Further up Norman Street lived the Eastmans. Their home was the meeting place and hangout for the "good time crowd" of Sandy Ground. There was lots of drinking and card playing. You could also depend on some number runner to come down into the woods and pick up your number bet. In those days you could play a number for five or ten cents. A quarter was heavy money. Sandy Ground can no longer boast of this down in the woods camaraderie. Oh yes, there would be arguments and fights, but by Monday morning everything was back to normal.

3090 ARTHUR KILL ROAD

This was the place to let it all hang out. If you wanted to find your spouse and they didn't come home, just get in touch with the Richardsons,

Kathleen or Jim. Barbecues started down there on many Friday, Saturday and Sunday nights. 3090 Arthur Kill Road, near Rossville, was the most well-known black home for boarders and transients. I recall a Miss Vivian living there and also a Mrs. Gilliam with her son James. Mrs. Gilliam sometimes attended our church.

Later Mr. Junius Nelson and Mrs. Helen Nelson took over 3090 but the reputation of the place did not improve. The Nelsons eventually bought a huge boarding house down in Tottenville.

GILBERT HENMAN, POOR DRIVER

Mr. Gilbert (Tobe) Henman, who lived on Clay Pit Road, was one of the worst drivers in the world. A community joke was that if you were a bad driver, you were labeled as driving like Mr. Tobe.

But he was always there as a volunteer to help our choir leader take us to various churches. His problem was that he never missed seeing something interesting, whether it was in front of him, on the side of him, or in the rear. Mr. Tobe, his wife Aunt Addie and their daughter Florence lived on Clay Pit Road. Mr. Tobe was related to Walter Henman, father of Geraldine McDonald.

JOHN HENMAN

Mr. John Henman, the Superintendent of the Sunday School, was one of the oldest residents of Sandy Ground. He used to hire himself out for plowing with his horses. He was good to us children. He would take us to Sunday School picnics in his horse and wagon and at times he took us for hayrides. He and his wife Mary had two sons, Lester and Japheth, and two daughters, Edna and Rachel. They lived on Crabtree Lane across from the cemetery and later on Winant Avenue. Edna Henman was the mother of Clayton Henman who, I later learned, was my half-brother.

If only we had a picture now of Mrs. Mary Henman, walking as fast as she could, one leg shorter than the other, and wearing such a long dress with so many petticoats under the dress. She hobbled and carried a cane. We children were in awe of her. She looked mean, but she really wouldn't hurt us. She would walk from Winant Avenue all the way to Pleasant Plains.

Ida Henman Gordon, who was born in Peekskill, N.Y., told me her mother's father John Tyler had been a slave. He worked for a good master who moved from New York to Boston. The master set John free.

A Postscript: Life Can Be Beautiful

Praise God from whom all blessings flow. "Jesus Keep Me Near the Cross" is my favorite hymn. If I lived to eternity I could not tell you all He has done for me.

Although I hardly knew what the word "dietitian" meant, soon after entering Tottenville High School I knew I wanted to be one. Food service became my goal. During my study periods and any other free time, I was assigned to work in the cafeteria. A government program paid us underprivileged kids for working. Today the program is called "Work Study." I learned a lot in the Tottenville High School cafeteria. Not only how to wash dishes in a machine, but also how to prepare and serve food. Mrs. Frances Kaltemeir, the head cook there, was very good to me. Mora Balfour (now Mrs. Eric Isbister, who lives in New Jersey) was my mentor.

After graduating from high school I worked during the summer at Camp Pratt, Prince's Bay, which was run by the YMCA of New York City. Miss Balfour then hired me to work in the Tottenville High School cafeteria. Although I was paid only $15 per week, she kept $5.00 out of my pay in her desk. The rest of my weekly salary I gave to my mother to help pay the family bills. I was given an allowance for carfare and lunch. Miss Balfour was a graduate of the Pratt Institute, Brooklyn. The money that Miss Balfour kept was used to pay my first tuition at Pratt.

I started out under Miss Balfour in 1946 as an assistant cook. Later I was under Rose Moore, head cook, and worked my way up to cook, dietitian and then consultant. For several summers I was assistant cook at Camp Pratt. I spent 11 summers at the Henry Street Settlement Camp

Cooks at Camp Echo Hill, near Peekskill, N.Y., 1947. *Rose Moore, Head Cook* (left) *and Lois Henry, Assistant Cook. Rose Moore lived in the Bronx. This was Lois's summer job while she was studying to be a dietitian at the Pratt Institute. Echo Hill was a camp of Manhattan's Henry Street Settlement.*

in Yorktown Heights, N.Y., and many summers at the boys' camp in Mahopac Falls, N.Y.

Although my mother passed away in 1948, she had the opportunity to share some of my experiences at Camp Echo Hill, near Peekskill, N.Y.

My whole family would visit me up at Yorktown Heights, only one hour away from the city. Uncle Kenny Landin usually drove Aunt Gert, Aunt Helen, my cousin Hayward Bevans, Estherlania Moore (wife of my cousin Calvin Moore), and all the others upstate. On my day off it was picnic time in the country for my family.

On Dec. 7, 1951, I married Glemby Mosley, a Sandy Ground boy I had known since childhood. He was born in Bayonne, N.J., but grew up in Sandy Ground. He lived with his foster parents, Kathleen and Jim Richardson, at 3090 Arthur Kill Road. Our wedding took place at Aunt Gert's house at 26 Clay Pit Road. Glemby had just come home from the army. During our high school years he had dated my sisters Mary Emily and Frances. He was an excellent athlete at Tottenville High School and also played with the local ball clubs. He enrolled in the army at about age 17. After the war a scout for the Black Yankees encouraged him to try out for the team and he played with them from 1946 to 1950, until the demise of the Negro League.

After marriage I continued working full-time at Tottenville High School. Later I worked at Willowbrook State School.

In 1953 I had an ectopic pregnancy which nearly cost me my life. I was employed at Willowbrook at the time and a friend brought me home from work quite ill. I was home alone at 569 Bloomingdale Road when I had an acute pain. I managed to crawl to the phone and call an ambulance. Al Hart and Freddie Carroll, co-workers at Willowbrook, came to the hospital after work to donate blood for me. I'll always be grateful to them.

I am the mother of six children, three boys and three girls: Glenda Beth (born Dec. 24, 1954), Gregory Alvin (Jan. 29, 1956), Gerald Stephen (Jan. 6, 1957), Gloria Ruth (Aug. 31, 1959), Gayle Etta (June 2, 1962) and Garret Francis (June 17, 1964). During the summer of 1954 at Camp Telfair, Ruth Tefferteller, the camp director, allowed me to bring Glenda and Gregory along and hired Amorie Bevans as a

Howard Kenneth Henry, ca. 1945. *Lois's brother in U.S. Army uniform. He served in the Philippines. His army paycheck supported the family for several years.*

Frances Henry (left), Calvin Moore, Lois Henry, ca. 1948. *Frances is Lois's younger sister. The group is seated on the concrete cover of the well at 569 Bloomingdale Road. In the background is the Rossville A.M.E. Zion Church. Calvin Moore, Aunt Frank's son, drowned in Round Pond in 1952.*

babysitter for them. Amorie selected the names of all my children, each one beginning with "G." While I worked at Maimonides Hospital, Hayward and Louise Bevans, who lived in Brownsville, Brooklyn, opened their home to me. I stayed in their apartment on days when I did not have 15 cents to get back home. The subway was a nickel. The ferry and the 113 bus also cost five cents each.

To my sister Mary Emily and my brother Howard I am grateful. They offered financial and emotional support during my most desperate times. After I married they never let my kids go hungry. They always shared their resources with me. Our love and caring for one another kept us close together. It does pay to be brought up in a Christian home.

God has been good to me. I could not then see into my future. How could a poor person like me go to college? Every time I needed money for tuition, by some miracle either Glemby or someone else would find a way to help me. On weekends I cooked and baked and sold my food to folks from the neighborhood. Once in a while the church would take up an offering to compensate me for playing for the choirs. The two or three dollars that they gave me helped to pay my carfare for the week. I never felt that I should be paid for services to my church. I was so poor I had to accept their offering. My tuition for a semester came to about $300. It cost $11 per credit. I paid my tuition on the installment plan.

After graduating from Pratt Institute with an associate degree, I found employment at Brooklyn's Maimonides Hospital, a strictly kosher hospital. Miss Ellen Mosley was the Senior Dietitian. I learned all I could about therapeutic diets from her.

After leaving Maimonides, I was given the opportunity to work at Willowbrook State School. I had put in an application before I went to Maimonidies. Willowbrook was closer to home. Dr. Glasser, the Personnel Director, hired me as an Assistant Dietitian. In those days you had to pass a psychological test and they took two weeks to check your background. At that time, about 1952, Willowbrook employees were the best that could be found. They could easily pick and choose whom they wanted to hire.

We had about 6,000 patients. Fred Carroll was Head Cook. Mr. Benjamin Gelbart was the Head Dietitian. He and I did not get along too well when I first started. The administration made him feel that eventually I would have his job. Politics! I did enjoy working at Willowbrook, although Fred Carroll manipulated me. I would order supplies and food but they would disappear. I therefore had to order more than was needed. I left to have a baby in 1954. They gave me a beautiful shower at the house of Mom Yuill, one of my colleagues. Then I came back to work and before I knew it, I was pregnant again.

In between my times of employment at Willowbook, I worked at St. Vincent's Hospital, as Floor Dietitian and for some time as Therapeutic Dietitian. I did have a few children in between! After six years in all at St. Vincent's, I finally left to give birth to my sixth child, Garret Francis. Sister Christopher wanted me to come back so bad that she said I could keep Garret under my desk!

With six children to care for, I did not seek re-employment at Willow-brook until 1965, returning there as Assistant Dietitian. Before Willow-brook would give me the title of Dietitian, however, they required me to go back to Pratt. In 1972, after 20 years' absence and six children, I earned my Bachelor of Science Degree, having managed also to make the Dean's List.

At Willowbrook, racial prejudice showed through all the phoniness. Miss Begley, from Great Kills, who read the Bible all day and was also Mr. Fred Carroll's neighbor, was given the job of Head Dietitian, although she only had an A.S. Degree. I was harassed over many years by the titles they gave me. One month I'd be a Dietitian, then Assistant, then Super-vising. With each title I carried the same work load, but it made my pay and grade rise and fall. At times I was supervising 300 employees.

Mr. Fred Carroll, Food Manager, was promoted to Food Administra-tor. He didn't even have a high school diploma. Mr. Elmer Hart was later promoted to Head Cook and then Food Manager. He didn't finish high school. I was the only one on the Food Service Administrative staff with a college degree to suffer such harassment.

During my years at Willowbrook, the name of the institution changed to the Staten Island Developmental Center. While there I made many lifelong friends. Especially Vada Castaldi, Artie Langilotti, Terry Berry, Sadie Sergeon and Florence Dombi. There were many more, but I am still in contact with the few I named.

In 1957 I moved to the Mariners Harbor housing project. Glenda, Gregory and Gerald were small children. My brood became too big for the little house at 569 Bloomingdale Road: there were only two bedrooms and no indoor toilet facilities. In the Mariners Harbor project our building was at 168 Brabant Street. Gloria was born there. With the arrival of Gayle and Garrett we needed more bedrooms and we moved within the same project to 169 Continental Place. We lived on the third floor between the Astwoods and the Wares. The Caldwells lived on the second floor as did Mary Ann Rowe. The Daniels lived on the first floor.

My sons are still friendly with many of the children they grew up with in the Mariners Harbor project. The Washington boys and the Harris boys were my sons' best friends. They all grew up as an extended part of our family. Mark Washington and his brother moved from the Mariners Harbor projects when we lived at 168 Brabant Street. Their apartment was next door to ours. The Harrises lived at 361 Grandview, also in the project. They later moved to the rear of our building at Continental Place. The Washingtons moved to the Bradley Avenue area known as "Dogpatch." Their mother still lives there.

Ma Betty Harris was a hard-working mom who raised her boys as a single parent. She was honored as a role model for the community. Her death in 1990 was sudden, even though she had many illnesses. She, my sister Mary Emily and I traveled all over with the high school and college basketball teams that our sons played on. Coach Pickman of the College of Staten Island always found room for us on the team bus. We were the senior cheerleaders. We had to pay for our own food.

Beneath us on Continental Place was the apartment of Mr. and Mrs. Robinson and their children, Donna, Michele, Robin and Lorraine. They were best friends of everyone then and now. They made up the female part of our extended family.

While living in Mariners Harbor, some of my kids had their start at the Port Richmond Nursery School. When it came Garret's turn, his older brother Gregory had the task of pulling and pushing him to go to school. When the day was over, it was just as hard to bring him home.

My children all attended P.S. 44. Mr. Quin was the most popular teacher. Later he became the principal. He was very strict, but respected. When Glemby had his accident, Mr. Quin and some of the teachers travelled to Manhattan's St. Vincent's Hospital to visit him.

After P.S. 44 my children attended P.S. 51, the Edwin Markham Junior High. Then to Port Richmond High School except for Gayle and Garret, who attended schools in Willingboro, N.J. Glenda and Gerry attended the College of Staten Island and Gayle attended Kean College. Garret also went to the College of Staten Island, where he and Gerry played on the basketball team. They were great athletes.

Greg entered the Marine Corps and later became a New York State Trooper, where he is at present a Senior Investigator. Gayle is a minister and teacher at an A.M.E. Zion school. Gerry is employed by the New York City Board of Education as a Security Officer. Glenda is a nurse's aide at St. Vincent's Hospital. Gloria is Assisant Director at the Burlington Recycling Company.

I am richly blessed in having great children. They are all employed. The boys don't smoke and are athletic. The girls are all mothers caring for their children. May God guide them and keep them and make them strong to be good role models for their children.

During the Christmas holidays when my children were young I worked at the post office in Brooklyn for about three weeks, from 11 P.M. to 7 A.M. Uncle Louis Pennyfeather, Evelyn Henry's husband, was Postmaster there. I also worked at Major's Fabric Store for six years, from 6 to 10 P.M. Mamie Daniels was my boss. My regular job was at Willowbrook from 8 A.M. to 4 P.M. Mr. Gilbert would make it convenient for me to take a little rest in between, when I was working three

Gregory and Elena Mosley and their children Tristan, Emel (front) and Glen-Paul (rear), Easter 1998. *Here the Mosleys pose in Sandy Ground after church. Mr. Hunter's house is in the background, on the left. One of the baymen's cottages is on the right. The Mosleys live in Claverack, Columbia County, N.Y. Gregory is a New York State Trooper Senior Investigator. They are founding members of Operation Unite, a social services organization of which Elena is Executive Director. Advocates of African arts, they founded Knumba Dance and Drum of Hudson.*

jobs. It was not easy for me to make money for my children's Christmas.

Finally, after many trials and tribulations, we were blessed with a way to move out of the Mariners Harbor projects into our own home. I did not want to leave Staten Island, but what realtors showed us was the dregs of Staten Island. Glemby was permanently disabled by an on-the-job accident at the New York City Department of Sanitation in 1970. He was hit head-on by a garbage truck while unloading his truck at the 14th Street dock in Manhattan, sustaining serious internal injuries. With the money he received as a settlement we were able to put a down payment on a home in Willingboro, N.J. Louise Grady Watkins, who lived there and also worked at Willowbrook, convinced me one day to ride home with her to Willingboro and I liked what I saw. For five years I rode up and down the New Jersey Turnpike to go to work. Illness forced me to retire on disability and take life a little easier.

During my early retirement I had a cooking class at the Rossville A.M.E. Zion Church. Each participant gave me ten dollars. For this they were able to make a main dish for their family and a dessert. The classes were greatly appreciated. The Sandy Ground Historical Society thought it would be a good community-relations project and took over sponsoring the classes, both children's and adult classes on Saturdays. It was a success for a while. I am not one to keep books or receipts and it became a hassle. During this time I was able to produce materials for two cookbooks. The Sandy Ground Historical Society has my material for a children's cookbook, which has not been published.

Today I am a happy retiree doing as I please with a few health restrictions. I love to travel and have been very happy doing just that. All my children have had the pleasure of travelling with me. Each year when I was at Willowbrook I would borrow from the Credit Union and have a payroll deduction. Just in time for my next vacation. I would do it all over again. I know that my children will never forget any of these experiences. My cousin Kenneth Landin Jr. was incarcerated for 15 years. When he had paid his dues to society and was released, Mary Emily and I gave the money for him to take a cruise.

Other than the ectopic pregnancy in 1953, I did not have any more medical problems until I went back to work at Willowbrook. I had managed to go through college and give birth to six healthy children without any illness.

Several years later my blood pressure became too high and I was diagnosed with congestive heart failure. I was forced to retire from Willowbrook in 1979. They gave me a farewell party and a trip to San Diego, Calif., to visit my daughter Gloria. Donald, her husband, was in the navy there. I took Garret, Gayle and Gerald with me on the plane. While in San Diego I experienced acute indigestion. It was diagnosed as congestive heart failure.

Shortly after retirement I became ill again from congestive heart failure. After moving to Willingboro I was admitted to the intensive care unit of the hospital there. After that episode I was declared disabled, unable to work. In 1988 while attending a birthday party for Miss Sis, I had a serious heart attack. At St. Vincent's Hospital the doctor in the emergency room did a tracheotomy on my neck. Thanks to him and God I am still living. On Sept. 12, 1988, they released me and sent me home. The next day I had a seizure and was rushed back to the hospital. Then home again and to the Cooper Hospital in Camden. I had the painful procedure to determine just what care I would need. It was done three times! I felt like I was on an assembly line waiting to be slaughtered. After a valve replacement and three months' hospitalization, I went home and was able to return to a normal life.

In 1994 a mammogram showed a malignancy that had to be removed. The operation to remove the tumor with half my left breast was performed in August. Because of my heart problem they could not put me under. They gave me a local anaesthetic but I could feel them snipping away at my breast. Following the operation, I had seven weeks of five-days-per-week radiation treatment. I did not like the radiologist. She seemed afraid to touch my skin. The girls who gave me treatment were great. The tattoos to mark the spots where I would receive radiation were fixed and are permanent. The greatest side effect, however, has been my hair. It is totally unmanageable. I was taught to do certain exercises to strengthen my arm muscles. Therapy was a must. All in all, I want to say, "Thanks be to God." He is good.

Most people have a secret fear in their mind that goes with them through their life. My fear has a mixed origin. The Landin family has a poor track record for living beyond 57 years. The Henry family historically lived to be 80, 90 or 100. I ask the Lord to bless me with a long productive life mixing the two bloods. So far I have passed the 75-year mark. I have a great desire to see my grandchildren develop and grow to do great things. Especially all to go to college. I would like to see my children as good parents guided by the Holy Spirit, training and loving their children and trying to be good role models.

PART THREE

Family Stories by
Other Sandy Grounders

Mom, Dad and Friends

BY THELMA "NAN" PEDRO

M Y parents were William "Pop" Pedro and Susan Jane Bishop
Pedro. I remember the night we moved to 36 Clay Pit Road. I
didn't like to ride in a car or truck. Everyone else was so happy they
jumped into the back of Pop's truck. Mom came back into the house to
see if everyone was out. One was still there. Guess who? Me! When Mom
found me, I was sitting in the corner. I did not want to ride in the truck.
Mom said that it wasn't going to hurt me. It would be only a short ride
and I finally went with the family.

When I lived at Clay Pit Road early we lost our sister Cora and later
our brother, Clarence Hyde. Even so, God was good to us in those days.
People had very little, but were happy with what they had. Now the more
they have, the more they want.

We had some happy times in that house. When I moved there I could
not walk. Everyone was so good to me. Even the outside kids. I walked
with a wooden cheese box because of a childhood disease. Pop would
bring the box home from work. Pop worked for a foodstore and a coalyard.

Our most happy times were in the basement of 36 Clay Pit Road. We
had a big round table and everyone had his own place at the table. Mom
and Pop got up at five o'clock every morning. They had to get the heat
up to warm the house. The fuels of the day were coal and wood. It was
nice and warm when we kids got out of the bed.

Mom gave me my first meal of the day at ten o'clock. When the kids
were out playing, Mom would bring us bread and jelly. At noon she had
the grandchildren and if we had other children playing with us, they had
lunch, too. I don't mean, bread and jelly and a glass of milk, we had a

William Henry Major "Pop" Pedro talking to schoolchildren, *Advance* photo, 1985. *"Pop" Pedro (1881-1988), who had retired as a truck driver and chauffeur, was appointed Sandy Ground's honorary mayor by Staten Island Borough President Ralph Lamberti in 1979. In this capacity he became an authority, receiving countless visitors, giving tours and often being interviewed in his home at 587 Bloomingdale Road. Alex Haley, author of* Roots, *visited him in 1986.*

whole meal every day. When she finished with us she would start supper. When evening came, she was so tired, she went to bed early.

Pop would eat his dinner and always leave something on his plate for us children. We all had our turn for this great treat. We didn't care what it was. We were happy because it came from Pop's plate.

Pop would often go outside and play ball with the kids. All the kids would come out and play with us: the Wallens, who lived next door; the Etheridges, Reillys and Gallaghers who also lived on Clay Pit Road. What good times we had! Pop, who was known as a cheater, never wanted to be called "Out."

Every day Pop would bring us and the grandchildren a piece of fruit home. On Saturday he would bring a small box of crackers home. On Christmas Day we would look for the crackers before we looked for other things.

On Saturday once a month, the men would go to other people's homes to play cards. You should see the food cooked for that night! They didn't leave their children home. The children were brought along and put to bed. My mom was a good singer. She would go around singing in other churches. Aunt Susie Henry and Aunt Frankie Moore would come to the card parties. They stayed all night. They fixed breakfast in the morning for everyone. The men always tried to see who could eat the most pancakes. Aunt Dora and my uncle would come up from the other side of the Island in their old Ford. I really can't remember all who came to these gatherings, but a good time was had by all.

The Pedros had a close-knit Sandy Ground family. They attended Rossville A.M.E. Zion Church, married in Sandy Ground and buried their dead there.

"Pop" Pedro at his 106th birthday celebration, Nov. 7, 1987. Standing behind "Pop" is Lucille Herring, his granddaughter. To the right is Julie Moody Lewis, his great-granddaughter. The occasion was the Ninth Annual Sandy Ground Proclamation Day Dinner, given by the Sandy Ground Historical Society at the Pavilion on the Terrace, New Brighton. Lois Mosley was honored for her contribution to the Sandy Ground community.

Memories

BY MARIE MOODY BOWERS

I remember Crabtree Lane and the schoolyard. That was our play ground. We made our own fun. We didn't have fancy slides and other playground equipment, but we used our imagination. We played all kinds of games: hide and seek, kick the can, mumblety- peg, and had all kinds of races, as well as baseball and football. Mr. Sarjeant often let us ride in his horse and buggy.

Once while we were playing, Mr. John Henman's horse grabbed my younger sister Thelma by the top of her head and dropped her. My, did Mr. Henman beat that horse!

Next to Stout's Candy Store, where we got two or three pieces of candy for a penny, we played ballgames in the field.

My father, Mose, made a swing for big girls and a little swing for smaller girls. My sisters Sylvia and Thelma and I were looked after by Aunt Nan. She baby-sat us at 27 Crabtree Lane across from the old P.S. 31. Aunt Ollie's boys used to help Aunt Nan. They never fussed, but the girls fussed and were bullies.

Aunt Nan used to take her baby-sitting money and buy herself new shoes. Perth Amboy, N.J., was the shopping place. You had to catch the 113 bus to Tottenville or go to the end of the Staten Island Rapid Transit to the ferryboat landing. Next you had to pay five cents to ride the ferry over to Smith Street in Perth Amboy. This to us was a great shopping place. It was only a few blocks long. Perth Amboy was a very prejudiced area, especially the eating places. Every week Aunt Nan used to buy a new dress. She had to look smart for the ballgame. We used to go down to Reinhardt's to watch our heroes play ball.

Mr. McCoy lived on Crabtree Lane. He was a stern, big, old man. We kids were in awe of him. I remember him saying, when we was angry, "You don't know your a— from your elbow." Cursing was a "no-no." He used to grab us kids with his hand that had two thumbs. He would squeeze our hands between those thumbs.

My dad used to bring home bags of clams. They would steam them open. Uncle Kenny Landin used to make the most delicious clam chowder. Mr. Jim Taylor and my father used to go hunting in upstate New York. They bagged a deer and it was the first time I tasted venison. Jim lived in Great Kills with his mother, Mrs. Lena Taylor. Jim's sister, Lucille, was married to Eddie Eaton. They attended our church. Mrs. Taylor was a very close friend of Mrs. Carrie Harris.

The Harris Family

BY MILDRED HARRIS ALLEN

Charles and Ethel Harris, my parents, have long been deceased. Their home at 624 Bloomingdale Road was an important place in Sandy Ground. Before moving to 624 Bloomingdale Road, their last residence, they lived at 144 Winant Avenue, then 570 Bloomingdale Road.

Ethel's father, John Mangin (1872-1937), came from New Jersey. Ethel's mother, Jane Mangin (1872-1937), was born in Maryland. John and Jane had eleven children: Ethel, Blanche, Amy, Mamie, Rosina, Hester, Joseph, Clarence, Floyd, Leon and Dennis.

Charles' father, Omer Harris, and his mother, Josephine Roach Harris, both came from New York City. Omer and Josephine Harris had five children: Charles, Ella, Edna, Augustine and Georgiana.

Ethel Mangin Harris was born in New York State on Nov. 4, 1891, and passed away on Aug. 6, 1955, at age 64. Charles Harris was born in

New York State on July 10, 1893. He passed away on Nov. 7, 1949 at age 56. They raised six children of their own and several children of relatives. Their children were: Gladys, Frances, Leonard, Mildred, Edith and Doris.

Ethel and Charles were known to the community for their spiritual education and uplifting example in the Rossville A.M.E. Zion Church. Charles was a construction worker and his last employment was as maintenance worker at the Halloran General Hospital for veterans. Ethel was an exceptional wife and mother and deeply rooted in the church. She was director of the church choir and leader of the prayer meeting. There was a friend that Ethel brought to Sandy Ground named Mrs. Ware. She was the reason why all the young people got saved and had the Holy Ghost. These were some lively times at the church! You had to be there. Ethel was a symbol of love for young and old. She arranged May Day parades, lawn parties, watermelon feasts and other types of entertainment for children of all ages.

In Sandy Ground anyone older than you was called usually "Aunt" or "Uncle," whether they were your cousin or not.

Aunt Ethel Harris dedicated her life to her family and to the Rossville A.M.E. Zion Church family. We usually had Junior Choir rehearsal on Wednesday nights. Sometimes we would meet at Aunt Ethel's house and she would be very generous. She gave us kids what she called a collation, cake and pudding or Jello or a glass of juice. Whatever she felt we deserved. Frances, her daughter, was the organist for the Junior Choir. Frances took her piano lessons from Aunt Gert.

Charles and Ethel also took children to the Bronx Park Zoo, Prospect Park Zoo, Central Park, beaches and many interesting places. They went mostly by public transportation. They took any child who wanted to go whether they were financially able or not. They also took truckloads of children and adults to different churches on Staten Island. It was these activities that brought peace and contentment to them as well as to others.

Charles and Ethel had only one son, Leonard, who remained at 624. He was called "Dutch" by everyone. He was born on Oct. 2, 1919 in Sandy Ground. "Dutch" attended P.S. 31 and P.S. 3. He was one of the few Sandy Grounders to go to McKee Vocational High School in New Brighton. During World War II "Dutch" saw action in Europe and the Philippines. He enjoyed life and can be remembered as a dedicated member of the Brown Bombers' Social and Athletic Club. "Dutch" was married and had three children. He also coached the girls' softball team. When "Dutch" died on Dec. 30, 1981, after a painful illness, his sisters thought a proper eulogy that summed "Dutch" up was the popular song, "I Did It My Way."

Cousin Gert Landin, my father's niece, was the musical director of Sandy Ground. She gave all the young people piano lessons. She travelled by foot from Sharrott's Road to everyone's house. Aunt Gert charged 50¢ an hour. Aunt Susie, Aunt Gert's sister, was the church organist before the Harris girls took over the choir. Aunt Susie was famous for making apple dumplings with or without sauce. They cost 15¢ each. They sure tasted good with homemade ice cream.

Mr. John Henman, the Sunday School Superintendent, used to sing, although he was not a singer. Our Sunday School picnics were always in Keansburg, N.J. Mr. John Henman owned a horse and wagon: that was his way of traveling. He did the plowing for the gardens in Sandy Ground. Mr. Henman went everyplace in that horse and wagon except to church. Mrs. Mary Henman, his wife, always wore long skirts that came to the heel of her shoes. You never saw her legs.

I remember the library on wheels, that came to church every two weeks. We were allowed three books at a time. It didn't last too long because not enough people participated.

Charles and Ethel's family grew and their children started families of their own. God was good to them in helping raise their children. The love continued in their lives to help whenever needed. If that kind of love existed today, the world would be a much better place. Today we children can look back and truthfully say it was our parents' footprints that we followed. They guided us through the sands of Sandy Ground to our present stages of life.

Memories of Sandy Ground
BY NORMA WALLEN McGHIE

Memories of growing up in Sandy Ground will always hold a special place in my heart. In life not all experiences are good, nor are they all bad, but I can truthfully say that the 17 years I spent in this community were mostly happy ones.

I was blessed with two beautiful parents who loved my brother Arthur and me very much and gave us a life of happiness. Dad was a little strict, but filled with a special love for his family and a desire to see us turn out as intelligent, well-mannered and loving individuals, well tuned into the right and wrong of any situation. Mom, Bertha Landin Wallen, was the most wonderful Mom in the world, as we often told her. She worked diligently with my dad, Alfred Wallen. Together they made our life beautiful.

I was born on Dec. 12, 1923. At that time we lived at 552 Bloomingdale Road, an address we refer to as the "old house." We lived there until I was six and one-half years old. There are certain things about the "old house" that I shall always remember. The house had two and one-half rooms downstairs, and two small rooms upstairs. It was cold in the winter and hot in the summer. There was no heat upstairs and no

Bertha Landin Wallen (Mrs. Alfred Wallen), ca. 1940. *Mrs. Wallen was a daughter of Robert H. Landin and Rebecca Gray Landin. Her husband Alfred, who worked on Wall Street, was born in Jamaica, West Indies. Their daughter is Norma Wallen McGhie, who contributed this chapter.*

fans anywhere. The kitchen was the only place where we could keep warm. I have memories of my mom sitting in front of the big stove in the kitchen with her feet in the oven! I remember hot summer nights in the upstairs rooms, but it seems that children can adapt to situations like that more than adults.

There were always visitors and laughter in the old house, in spite of its many inconveniences. At that time we didn't have a bathroom in the house. We had what was referred to as an outhouse in the backyard. How we hated that place! Sometimes rather than go to the outhouse, we held back and became constipated. We had to take castor oil. We soon made up our minds that the outhouse was the lesser of two evils, even if snakes were around there.

Dad was very concerned that we learn ABCs and numbers before we started school. Every Sunday afternoon he would put up the blackboard and teach my brother Arthur and me. Also on Sunday afternoons after dinner, Dad would take us all for a ride and maybe stop at a roadside stand and buy us treats, ice cream and frankfurters. Al Deppe's on Arthur

Kill Road near Richmond Avenue in Greenridge was the most popular place. Mother loved Jack's Idle House on Richmond Avenue in Greenridge, too. Their soft- shell crabs were unforgettable.

The Henry family lived on one side of us and Uncle Jimmy Decker lived on the other. Lois and Howard Henry were our playmates. I remember my dad would always bring candy home for "little Lois," as he called her. Howard and I were the same age and Lois was a few years younger. My brother Art was a year older than I was.

While we were still living in the old house, Mom and Dad decided to have a new house built for us. I shall never forget the day we moved into our brand-new house. I felt like a princess moving to a palace. The date we moved in was August 14, 1930. We had three lovely rooms downstairs, three bedrooms upstairs, a nice basement and a big front porch and best of all, an inside bathroom. Our new address was 26 Bogardus Avenue, later known as Clay Pit Road. Our neighbors were the Pedros next door. Across the street lived the Moodys and the Henmans. Down the road a bit were the Etheridges and Mr. Fred Roach and his mom.

We loved our new home. I had my own room and also the basement to play house in. We played with the Pedro family and Mr. Pedro often played baseball with us. I became good friends with Thelma ("Boots") and Isabel Etheridge. My brother Arthur played with Wendel Etheridge ("Jiggs"). We all attended P.S. 31, a one-room schoolhouse (although the room could be divided into two), grades one to three. We loved that little school, with one teacher. To this day, I feel very sad when I pass by and realize the school burned. After third grade, we attended P.S. 3 in Pleasant Plains. The bus picked us up on the corner of Clay Pit Road and Bloomingdale Road every morning at 8:30 and brought us back home at 3:15.

My mother worked four days a week. I remember how excited and happy we were when we came home from school on her day off. She was always there to greet us. The house had a certain warmth and glow that it didn't seem to have when she wasn't there. The other days of the week we were "latch-key kids," by today's description, but it was only for two hours. Mom always came home at five o'clock. She then had to rush, prepare dinner and meet Dad at the Pleasant Plains train station in our Chevy at 6:00 P.M.

I recall eating all our meals in the dining room, which also contained my piano. I took lessons from Miss Gertrude Landin, who was the local piano teacher and also my mother's third cousin. The lessons cost 50¢ an hour. Part of me wanted to play the piano and the other part hated the lesson and the hour I had to take from my playtime everyday to practice. I took lessons for three years and at the age of 15, I would play on alternate Sundays for Junior Choir. Lois Henry also played and was much better than I was, in my opinion.

Mrs. Charles (Ethel) Harris was in charge of the Junior Choir at the Rossville A.M.E. Zion Church. We all adored her. She was always so patient and would take us on picnics and do those things that are special to children. She really cared about us.

I remember the fights I had with the other children. They liked me and I always had playmates, but they also liked to pick fights with me. My main sparring partners were Dora Moody and Isabel Etheridge. In spite of it all, we remained good friends. All the kids loved to play at my house because we had a big sidewalk in front that was perfect for roly-poly and hopscotch. Also the front steps were good for "Upstairs, Downstairs."

I think the place where we had the best times was in my basement. It was my domain! I had it fixed up like a little living room with my mom's old furniture and curtains. I remember the plays Boots Etheridge and I put on. I would write the play and Boots and I rehearsed the parts and then we would scout around and get all the little kids in the neighborhood whose mom would give them two cents' admission to see our play. Sometimes we made as much as twenty cents. After the play we would dismiss the kids and go up to Millie Stout's Candy Store to spend the loot. When my dad found out what we were doing, he gave me a sound spanking and told me never to charge admission again. Believe me, we didn't. I loved performing just for the sake of acting. I aspired to be a dramatic actress.

When I reached my teen years we used my basement for our jitter-bug sessions. We formed a club called "The Marvelettes," and we met in my basement every Friday night to jitterbug. We had an old Victrola and started with three records, which we built up to quite a few. One of these records was "Tuxedo Junction." The members of our club were my brother and me, Bill Pedro, Edith and Millie Harris, Daisy and Elmer Cooper, Kip Henry, Lindwood and Lenora Moore. We had so much fun! I think all my friends felt sad when we moved to Manhattan in September 1941.

I attended Tottenville High School from the ages of 13 to 17 and graduated in January 1941. There were never more than six or seven black students during my four years in high school. I had known Daisy Cooper all my life but did not really get to be in her company much until we attended high school. She and I became best friends and did every-thing together and even dressed alike when we went on excursions or on bus rides to Coney Island. We graduated and shortly after, my family moved to Manhattan. We corresponded and spoke on the telephone. Daisy would come and spend occasional weekends with us at our apart-ment on Edgecombe Avenue in Washington Heights. After graduating from Tottenville High School, I attended Brooklyn College.

Daisy married before I did. I was her maid of honor and godmother to Debbie, her firstborn. I married a couple of years later and she was my matron of honor and godmother to Sherri, my firstborn. Ours is a spe-cial friendship which has lasted down through the years and has grown deeper. We have been best friends since 1941. We have a great deal of love and respect for each other that only grows richer as time goes by.

I am a descendant of the Landin family. My grandfather was Robert H. Landin, an oysterman from Talbot County, Maryland, and an early settler of Sandy Ground. He was a kind, soft-spoken, religious man, a local preacher in the church. He and his wife Rebecca had 12 children, but six died in infancy or early childhood. They raised six children to adulthood: Arlene Landin Decker, Grace Landin Mitchell, Sam Landin, Bertha Landin Wallen (my mother), Maude Landin and Vera Landin Usry.

My grandmother, Rebecca Landin, was born in Manhattan. Her maiden name was Gray. She had one sister, Jennie, and three brothers, Ben, Stephen and Walter. Grandma only had a grammar-school education, but she became quite a businesswoman. She owned at least three different houses in the community. When I was a youngster, she would take me with her as she went around and collected rent from the people who lived in her boarding house on the corner of Woodrow Road and Bloomingdale Road. The Landin family homestead at 1482 Woodrow Road is still standing. It is now occupied by Gwendolyn Mitchell and her son David. It's still all in the family. Gwen was married to my cousin Robert, who is now deceased.

So many memories run through my mind as I think of the Landin homestead where my brother Art and I spent a lot of time visiting and playing. They had a big yard with apple trees, peach and pear trees, and grapevines. Grandpop always had a garden. We had a swing that he made us and a seesaw on an old tub in the backyard. Grandpop kept chickens and we would watch as he killed a chicken every Saturday for Sunday dinner. He read the Bible a lot and would sometimes read passages to us. I loved both Grandma and Grandpop, but Grandpop was very special to me. He died when I was ten years old, and I was deeply affected by his death. I wrote a poem which was read at his funeral and then it was discovered that I had a talent for writing poetry.

My Aunt Arlena lived at 1498 Woodrow Road, next door to my grandparents' house. She was married to Abram Decker and had two children, Elmer and Mabel.

Mabel married Bromley Munro, who was originally from the British West Indies. They had two children, Marcia and Herbert. Mabel continued to live at home after she married Bromley, better known as Mannie. Mannie was an iceman, but had a passion for raising dahlias. His flowers won first prize at all the flower shows on Staten Island. He decided to give up his job delivering ice and to spend all of his time growing flowers. He had two greenhouses put up on his property and raised chrysanthemums. He made out very well in this venture and soon people came from all over Staten Island to buy his flowers. Unfortunately, he died at the age of 72 from a heart condition. Mabel continued in the flower business until she became ill. Marcia is still living on Staten Island. Herbert resides in Jackson, N.J., with his wife Joyce.

My Aunt Grace married Fritz Mitchell from Rye, N.Y., and had two sons, Benjamin and Robert. Uncle Sam never married. He lived with Aunt Grace and Uncle Fritz in Rye. He was a good man. He would give anyone the shirt off his back. He loved to write poetry. It was his hobby. Benjamin and Robert Mitchell are now deceased.

Aunt Arlie and Uncle Abe, like all the Landin family, were very devoted to the Rossville A.M.E. Zion Church. She was the church treasurer for many years. Uncle Abe was director of the Senior Choir. I can still remember him singing solos in his rich tenor voice. Aunt Arlie and also my mother Bertha were members of the Stewardess Board and other groups at the church. They are all deceased.

My grandmother Rebecca would come to church every Sunday and sit in the middle pew, third seat on the aisle. She always dressed in the long dresses, with lace and finery, that seemd to come from another era.

Maude Landin, Rossville A.M.E. Zion Church, 1995. *Miss Landin, who contributed a chapter to this book, was a daughter of Robert H. Landin and Rebecca Gray Landin. She was the oldest member of the church.*

What hats she wore! She was a very stylish woman.

The Landin family was a very proud family and at the same time, very down to earth. I am proud to be a descendant of the Landin family.

My mother Bertha married my dad, Alfred Wallen, who was born in Jamaica, British West Indies. They had two children. My dad worked at the New York Stock Exchange on Wall Street for many years. He was a good provider for his family. He had a brother, Arthur, to whom he was deeply attached. Uncle Arthur lived in New York City. He is now deceased.

Aunt Vera married William Usry and had one daughter, Yvonne. My brother and I were in Aunt Vera's company more than that of any of our aunts and we loved her dearly.

Aunt Maude never married, but had a lot of nieces and nephews, family and otherwise. She was everybody's Aunt Maude. I remember when we were young it was always Aunt Maude who took us to the museums, Radio City Music Hall and so many interesting places. She was very special to us. She died at age 100 on September 10, 2002.

There is so much I could write about of my years in Sandy Ground, but that would be a book in itself. I would like to list a few of the events that were part of our young lives in Sandy Ground: Sunday School pic-nics every year at Keansburg, N.J.; hayrides; bus rides to Coney Island; baseball games at Reinhardt's; Children's Day at church; Christmas par-ties; trick or treating; roller-skating and playing at P.S. 31; tent revivals; Stout's Candy Store; Wolfe's Pond Park swimming and picnicking; the Memorial Day parade in Pleasant Plains; Mr. Fred Roach's tennis courts; the ice-skating pond on Clay Pit Road; John P's ice cream truck; the ragpicker and the gypsies.

At age 17, six months after I graduated from high school, my family had a financial setback. My dad lost his job of 20 years at the New York Stock Exchange. He had to look for another job. He worked at the Nassau Smelting Company for a while. He decided it was not for him. My par-ents decided it would be better to give up our home on Staten Island. We moved to 155th Street and Edgecombe Avenue in Washington Heights, Manhattan. It was traumatic in one sense, but adventuresome, in another. I will not dwell too much on this part of my life because this story is about Sandy Ground. I'll sum it all up by saying we found life very pleas-ant in New York City. Of course, we never forgot our roots.

My mother died in 1952. She was only 52 years of age. My dad lived to the age of 88 and died on Oct. 26, 1990. I was very close to him and I miss them both very much. I know they are with God and their spirits and memory will always be with us.

I married Lloyd McGhie in 1953. He was born in Jamaica, British West Indies. We have two daughters, Sherri and Gail; two granddaugh-ters, Nicole and Adrienne; and one great-granddaughter, Payton. We live in Edgewater Park, N.J. We like it very much but I shall never forget Sandy Ground.

Memories

BY MAUDE LANDIN

I would like to write a brief summary of my family life growing up in Rossville. I was one of 12 children, two of whom were twins. Unfortunately four children died in infancy. Cora died at the age of four and Irving died at 16. Six children lived to maturity: Samuel, Arlene, Grace, Bertha, Maude and Vera.

My father Robert H. Landin was a devout Christian. He was a kind, gentle, loving man, who was always concerned about his family and friends. He studied for the ministry and was ordained. He was qualified in every aspect for the ministry. The bishop offered him a small church in Rahway, N.J., but he refused it because he had no desire to uproot his family. He wished to remain as a member of the Rossville A.M.E. Zion Church, assisting the pastor when needed, without salary.

He was special with his children. He raised them in a Christian atmosphere and spent time making different toys and playthings for them: whittling wooden sticks, making hoops from old bicycle tires, swings, jump ropes, seesaws, etc. In this way we kept occupied at home and had no need to run to other kids' homes for fun. We all loved him very much.

My mother Rebecca Landin was a very stylish woman and also very religious. She was the disciplinarian in our home. She assigned special duties to us girls which she expected us to follow. She was always concerned about our health and welfare. We were always well fed. She made our clothing and sometimes sat up all night in order to finish a dress for a special occasion.

Mother was strict about our schooling and advancement. She bought a piano so that all the girls could take lessons. The neighbor who taught us played well but was not a good teacher. She only charged 30¢ per half

LEFT: Robert H. Landin, ca. 1930. *Collection of Norma Wallen McGhie. An oysterman originally from Talbot County, Maryland, Robert H. Landin (1854-1934) was a trustee of the Rossville A.M.E. Zion Church and a local preacher. Here he appears to be holding a Bible. He was the father of Maude Landin and grandfather of Norma Wallen McGhie and Yvonne Usry Taylor.*

RIGHT: Rebecca Gray Landin (Mrs. Robert H. Landin), ca. 1940. *Collection of Norman Wallen McGhie. Mrs. Landin (1863-1955) is admiring the dahlias in Bromley Munro's garden at 1498 Woodrow Road. She and her husband lived at 1482 Woodrow Road. An enterprising woman, she owned many Sandy Ground rental properties in the 1930s and 1940s. Her parents, Stephen and Martha Gray, were from Manhattan, where Rebecca was born.*

hour but she always seemed so tired that she often nodded off and I would skip a page. What a brat!

I was the dreamer in the family. The main parts of my life were the church and the other young people in the community. In addition to the religious guidance, plays, musicals and concerts took place every week or so at church. We had seven-cent dinners, which consisted of franks and beans. The Henry family were very musically inclined and all good singers. My family, the Landins, were not singers, but were good at reading or reciting poetry.

Before the church was at its present location, it was located in the cemetery further down Bloomingdale Road. It was a small building. When the congregation moved to the new church, we used the old church for entertainment. One night we had a prizewinning cakewalk contest. I was about four or five years old and fell asleep. When it was over, the lights were put out and everyone left. After walking a short distance, my mom missed me. She had thought I was with one of my sisters. Not so! They rushed back to the church and found me asleep in the corner. If I had awakened before they came back, there would have been another small grave there.

The highlights of the year were revival meetings in the winter, camp meetings in the summer for about six weeks, and other entertainment all year, including weddings, formal dinners, and ballgames on Saturday afternoons. Howard Henry Sr. was the star of Sandy Ground ballgames. He was an excellent pitcher. He would have qualified for the major leagues today. I recall during our church revivals all my friends would go up to the mourners' bench (for repentant sinners). I went there twice and I didn't get the Holy Spirit the way they did until my third trip. I had planned to fake it but miraculously something came over me and I jumped up in the air and felt as light as a feather. It was a beautiful feeling.

As regards my love life while a teenager, I fell in love with Theodore Roach. On Sept. 7, 1918, my sister Grace gave birth to my nephew Benjamin Mitchell. That same morning I walked to the corner to get the bus for high school, but when I got on the bus I noticed all the children looked sad. I asked them what was the matter. They told me that Theodore had the flu and he died that morning. I said, "Oh, My God!" I was crushed at the age of fifteen and one-half years.

Now at the age of 89 I look back at that time in my life, with my family and friends as a wonderful experience and a time to be cherished and remembered.

My Life and Family

BY MALVINA MOODY TEMPLE

My mother, Ella Harris Moody, and my father, Charles Moody, lived with my maternal grandparents, Omer Harris and Josephine Roach Harris, at 624 Bloomingdale Road. I was one of six children. Our parents and grandparents came originally from the Eastern Shore of Maryland.

When I was about seven years old my mother left our family and moved to New York City. She took my youngest brother, Lester, with her. My father at the time was working on an oyster boat. He was often away from home. When he returned home he found that my mother had gone and that she had left four of us children with our grandmother. Gladys, my older sister, was working. Harold, Milford, Christopher and I were in school. My father removed us from school and placed us in a Children's Aid Society home.

He and Mother had a bitter fight in court over the custody of the children. My mother was allowed to keep Lester. Milford, Harold and Christopher were returned to my grandmother. I was taken to live with a Mrs. Barrigher in Tottenville. I stayed there only for a while then went to the city to live with my mother.

My mother married Wally Hood and they had two sons, Bernard and Leroy. She died in 1928 while giving birth to a third son. He did not live.

After my mother died I lived with my Aunt Augustine in New York City and with whomever else would give me a place to stay. I knew very little about taking care of myself. I was only 14 years old when my mother died. After I was shuttled around from pillar to post for about three years, my sister Gladys came to Manhattan and brought me back to Staten Island, where I have been ever since.

When I came back to Staten Island I had one child and was pregnant with another. I stayed with Gladys for about three or four years. She moved to Port Richmond and I had to find a place for me and Marion and Robert, my two children. I got a room in a house in back of the cemetery on Crabtree Lane. I lived there until I met Charlie Temple, a Sandy Ground resident who had been born in Virginia. Charlie and I became good friends and got married. We had six children: James, Alvin, Charlotte, Richard, Ronald and Melvin.

Things were hard in those days. Charlie worked for the W.P.A. When we were on welfare Charlie got a job at the National Pneumatic Co. in New Jersey. He then went to work in construction until he retired.

I was working days at Sea View Hospital and Home until I retired on disability in 1974. While working at Sea View I took the G.E.D. test and got my high school diploma. I then took a 16-week course at the College of Staten Island and received a diploma. I took the clerk's test and passed that too. I accomplished all of this after I was 50 years of age.

Charlie died in 1971 and I went to California with my oldest daughter Marion, staying there for six weeks. When I returned to Staten Island I stayed with my youngest daughter Charlotte because I did not want to live alone. Each of my children has given me grandchildren: Marion and Charlotte each have two girls; Richard has two boys and two girls; Ronald has two boys and one girl; and Melvin has one girl and one boy. Altogether I have 23 grandchildren and 14 great-grandchildren!

I am a member of the Rossville A.M.E. Zion Church in Sandy Ground as were my parents and grandparents. I love to sing and am a member of the choir. I was President of the Pastor's Aid Society for fourteen and one-half years. I am now the Treasurer of the Pastor's Aid Society and the Men's Club. I enjoy working in the church and I love Bible study.

There is not much I can do now, because I have severe arthritis.

After retirement I went to California to visit Marion, Robert and Ronald, who live there. Robert and Ronald were in the U.S. Navy and Marion's husband Earl was also in the U.S. Navy. Each made a career in military service. I enjoy cruising and have been on many cruises to the Caribbean. My most enjoyable trip was traveling with a group from my church across country to California.

Now I live in a senior citizens' complex in New Brighton and travel back and forth to my church in Sandy Ground. In the senior citizens' complex we have lots of activities to keep us young such as bingo, bridge, trips to Atlantic City and shopping trips. We all celebrate our birthdays in the proper month. I enjoy going to Willingboro, N.J., to visit my cousin Lois Mosley.

A grandmother's love is greatly increased because of her great-grandchildren's love. Robert is nine years old, Temea is eight; Lauren is five, and Matthew is four. They are the offspring of my granddaughter Lynn. My son Richard's grandchildren are babies. I'll have to wait a while to get to know them. Alvin has one granddaughter who lives in Queens. Her name is Tonya and she is six years old. My oldest daughter Marion has three grandsons. James, who is deceased, has four grand-children.

I thank God for all that he has done for me. My life started out shaky, but thanks to God and a loving family in my senior years I am able to enjoy a full and reasonably healthy life.

PART FOUR

Street by Street

Sandy Ground Buildings and Their Photographers[†]

A remarkably complete photographic record of Sandy Ground's buildings as they stood ca. 1940 is preserved through the NYC Tax Department photographs now housed in the Municipal Archives. They are frontal shots of individual buildings from the street, but never including the occupants. Apparently taken in winter or early spring, they offer maximum visibility of the buildings and the surrounding bare landscape. The tax block and lot numbers are prominently displayed on a sign in front of each property. Individual photographers are not identified.

In most cases, these are the only surviving images of buildings that no longer exist.

William T. Davis, Staten Island's well-known naturalist and historian, took several photographs of Sandy Ground in the 1930s. Some are labeled "Africa," but without specific street addresses. The houses represented were probably located in or near Harris Lane, the earliest part of Sandy Ground, called "Harrisville."

Three other photographs included here were taken in 1927 by Staten Island resident Percy Loomis Sperr (1889-1964), a professional photographer. His collection of 25,000 New York City views now resides in the New York Public Library. In later years he was the proprietor of a

---

[†] *The photographs which follow are arranged by street in ascending order by house number. Bloomingdale Road, with the largest number of buildings, is presented first by west side, then by east side. Clay Pit Road is divided by north and south. Unless otherwise stated, all photographs are from the New York City Department of Records & Information Services, Municipal Archives, ca. 1940. Annotations are by Lois Mosley and Barnett Shepherd.*

bookstore on Victory Boulevard, Tompkinsville. His sharp artistic images are carefully labeled by street and give ownership of the properties photographed.

For the most part, Sandy Ground's houses are no different in type from many other houses built during the 19th century throughout Staten Island. They are wood frame dwellings with straight gable roofs, end chimneys and clapboard or shingle siding. The gable end faces the street, or the gable ends are on the sides.

These houses are nearly always three bays wide. Bays are structural openings, either windows or doors. On Staten Island the door of a three-bay house is never in the middle, but on one side or the other. It opens into a stair hall. Off the hall is the main living space, often two rooms. The kitchen is in the basement or on the ground floor in the rear, in the body of the house or in a lean-to. Upstairs are two or three bedrooms.

The Newton residence, 1546 Woodrow Road, and the Buehl residence, 1530 Woodrow Road, two of the earliest houses in the area, were built as three-bay houses but were later converted into five bays. The Prasse farmhouse, 535 Bloomingdale Road, and the Landin brothers' residences, 183 and 187 Sharrott's Road, are other examples.

Another early building, 15 Harris Lane, probably began life around 1850 as a three-bay house. The addition of a two-bay section on the right converted it into five bays. This is called by tradition the "Wood Peg House." It may have been built by Silas Harris or Moses Harris, two of Sandy Ground's earliest black settlers, but the earliest houses were mostly built and occupied originally by whites.

In the 1890s, Sandy Ground's most prosperous era, African Americans built fashionable new houses on Bloomingdale Road. These houses were in the Colonial Revival, Queen Anne, and Bungalow styles. These include 444, the Isaac Harris residence; 548, the Francis Henry residence; and 624, the Omer Harris residence. By 1897, with the completion of the new Rossville A.M.E. Zion Church, Bloomingdale Road had become the main street.

The Pedro-Herring residence, 36 Clay Pit Road, and the Moody residence, 40 Clay Pit Road, were built in 1923 and 1924 respectively in the popular Bungalow style. The Bevans residence, 591 Bloomingdale Road, and the Wallen residence, 26 Clay Pit Road, were put up in 1930. (These three dates were found in Dept. of Buildings records.) These houses represent the end point in Sandy Ground domestic architecture built for African Americans, who had by then become suburbanites.

Lois Mosley has provided information on the occupants of these houses from her knowledge and experience of the community over the decades. Her fellow parishioners of the Rossville A.M.E. Zion Church, especially Yvonne Taylor, have been helpful. Maps and atlases have provided primary information. No attempt has been made to establish a detailed record of the each building's ownership. Where specific historical information is given, sources are cited. It is hoped that the publication of this book will elicit more information.

—BARNETT SHEPHERD

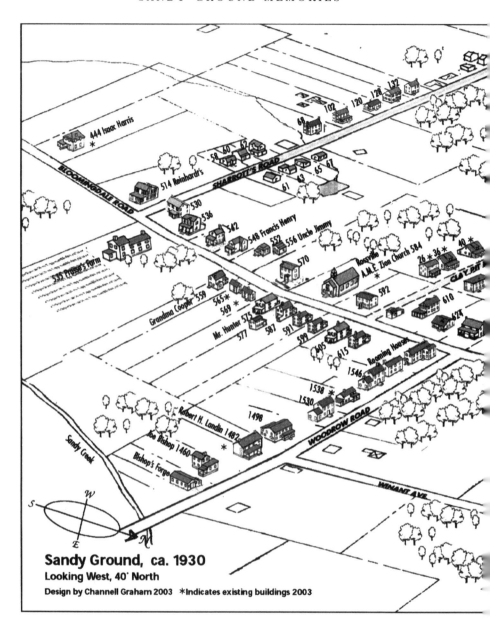

444 Isaac Harris *
514 Reinhardt's
BLOOMINGDALE ROAD
SHARROTT'S ROAD
58 60 62
65 67
63
61
530
536
542
548 Francis Henry
552 556 Uncle Jimmy
570
533 Prosser's Farm
Grandma Cooper 559
565 *
569 *
Mr. Hunter 573
577 587
591
599
605
615
102
120 128 132
68
Rossville
A.M.E. Zion Church 584 *
26 * 36 * 40 *
592
CLAY PIT
610
624
Rooming House
1546
1538 *
1530
1498
Robert H. Landin 1482
Joe Bishop 1460
Bishop's Forge
*
WOODROW ROAD
WINANT AVE
Sandy Creek
W
S
E
N

Sandy Ground, ca. 1930
Looking West, 40° North
Design by Channell Graham 2003   *Indicates existing buildings 2003

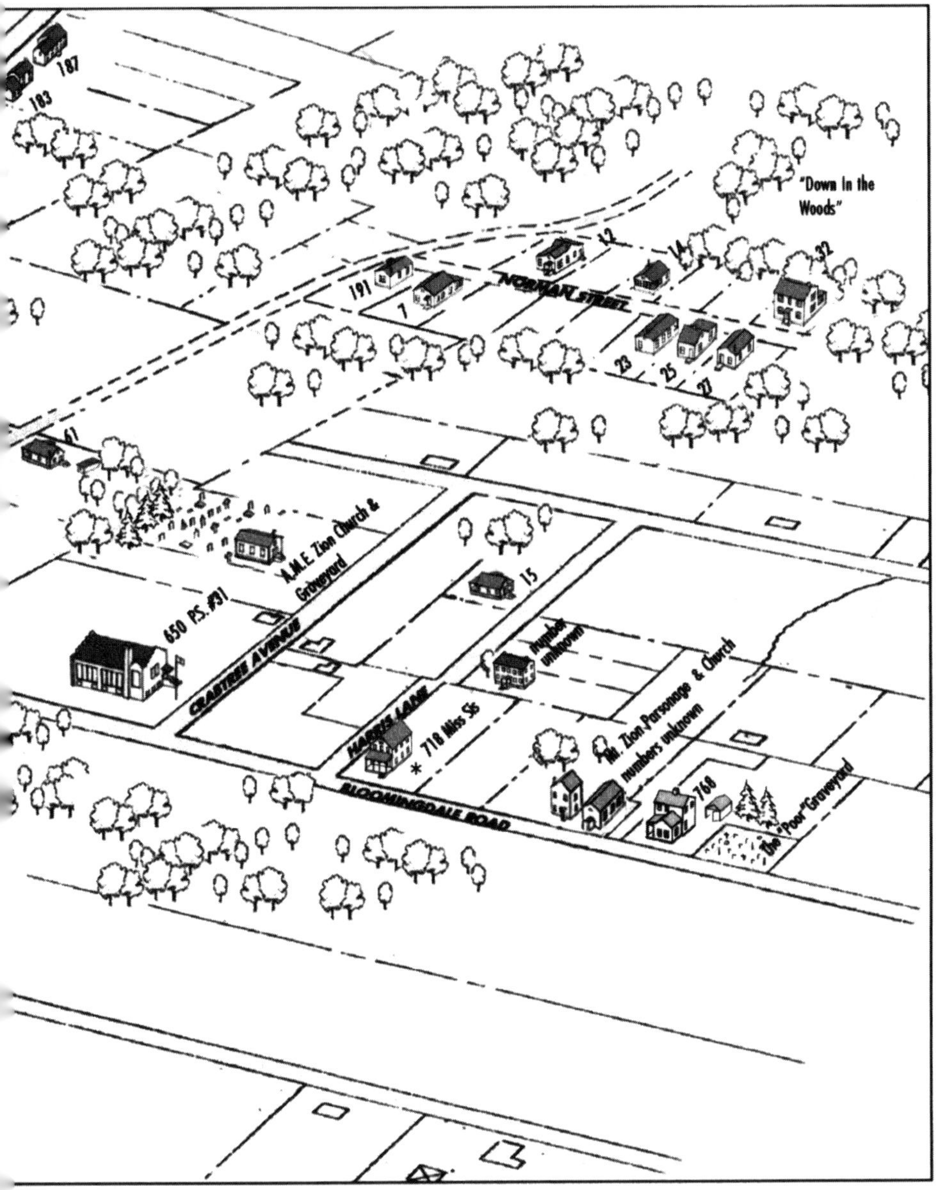
187
183
"Down In the Woods"
12
14
32
191
7
NORMAN STREET
23
25
27
61
A.M.E. Zion Church & Graveyard
15
650 PS. #31
CRABTREE AVENUE
number unknown
Mt. Zion Parsonage & Church numbers unknown
HARRIS LANE
* 718 Miss S&
768
The "Poor" Graveyard
BLOOMINGDALE ROAD

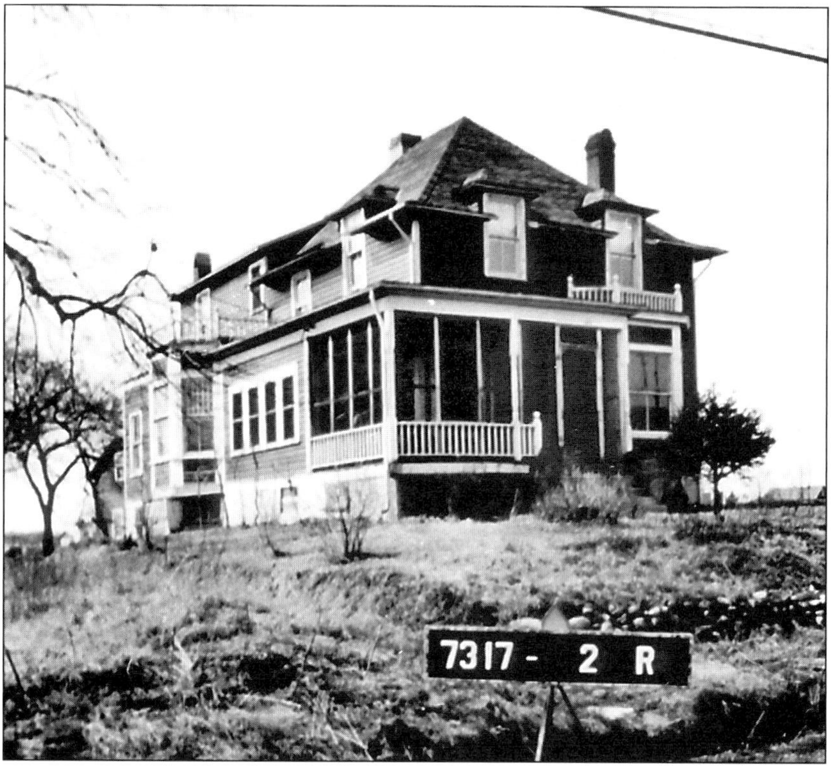
7317 - 2 R

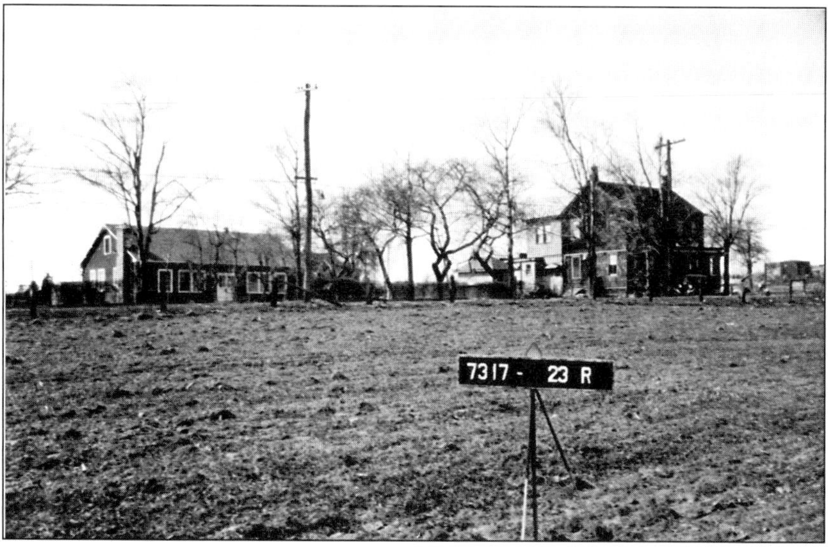
7317 - 23 R

Bloomingdale Road: West Side

444 Bloomingdale Road, Isaac Harris House

Built for Isaac Harris, after he purchased the land in 1896, this eclectic Colonial Revival house is the most sophisticated residence in the neighborhood. Isaac Harris was employed in domestic service by Stanford White (1853-1906), the famous architect. According to Harris, as quoted in several sources, White assigned two employees from the firm of McKim, Mead and White to design this house. The docket book in the Building Department of Borough Hall, however, indicates that the house was designed by Emery Roth and built in 1898. Roth (1871-1948), now famous as the architect of many New York City skyscrapers, immigrated from Hungary in 1893. After working as a draftsman, in 1898 he established his own practice. The Isaac Harris house would rank as one of his earliest works. It still stands.

514 Bloomingdale Road

This was the Reinhardt's of Lois's childhood and adolescence, "an amusement park for white folks." The building on the right housed the restaurant; the building on the left, originally a barn, had been converted into a picnic shelter. The ballpark was behind the two buildings. Emil and Johanna Reinhardt, German immigrants, purchased the property in 1911. They opened a restaurant there, "The Neighbor." Their specialty was knockwurst with German potato salad. By the 1950s, there were three pool tables and dancing to a juke box. (Source: Joseph Mitchell's notes, SIIAS.)

White Staten Islanders found this a popular place of entertainment. Picnics, ballgames and other sporting events were held on the four-acre grounds. In the front section of the building on the right was the bar and in the rear the restaurant. The owners resided upstairs. There was a candy store on the Sharrott's Road side of the building.

Sandy Ground blacks entered through the rear door. They were allowed to purchase candy and liquor but not allowed to eat there. During the 1930s Sandy Ground children came to the picnic and ballgrounds to watch, entertain and beg.

The Eagle Athletic Club, a black baseball team starring Howard Clayton Henry, Lois's father, played other Staten Island teams here. Black teams, white teams, and integrated teams all played together here and in other Staten Island locales (Askins, 1988, p. 123).

Sleepy Hollow Inn

SIIAS photograph, 1979. Margaret Sklenar purchased the restaurant portion of the property in 1967. Herman Reinhardt, son of Emil and Johanna Reinhardt, continued to operate the business while living there with his wife Hilda. When Herman died in 1971, his wake took place in the restaurant. In 1972 Mrs. Sklenar became the manager, renaming the business "The Sleepy Hollow Inn." Its popularity continued. Black Sandy Grounders were employed by Mrs. Sklenar and allowed to eat there for the first time. The grounds were popular for weddings. The property was sold to a developer in 1988 and the building was demolished in 1989. Townhouses have recently been built on the site.

530 Bloomingdale Road

The Charles Logan family lived here in Lois Mosley's childhood. The house is located at the corner of Sharrott's Road and may have been the original Sharrott family residence. A house marked "W. B. Sharrot" appears in this location on Beers' atlas of 1874. To the right of the house is seen a carriage house with dovecote.

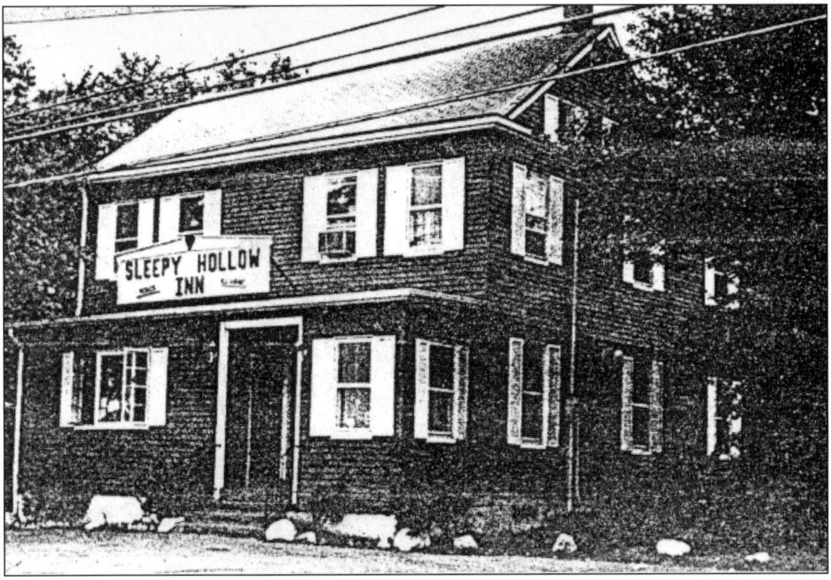
SLEEPY HOLLOW
INN

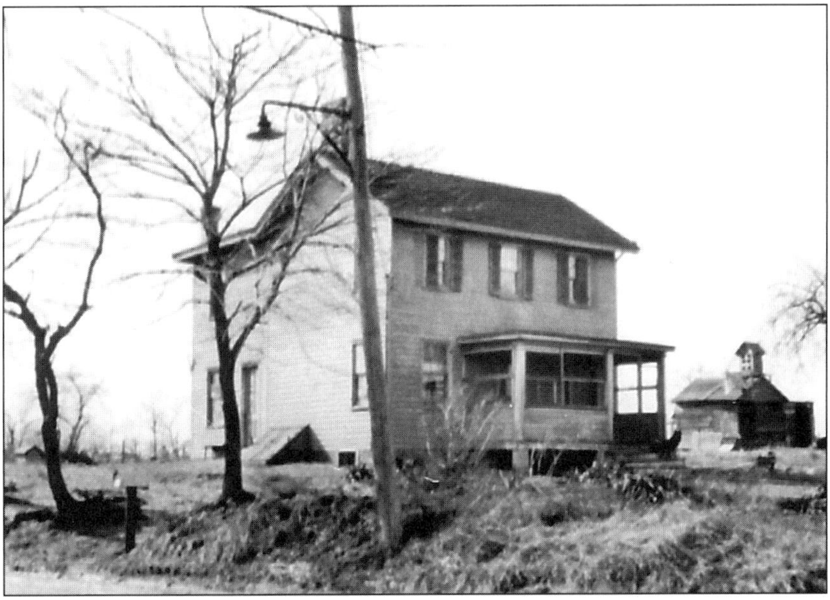

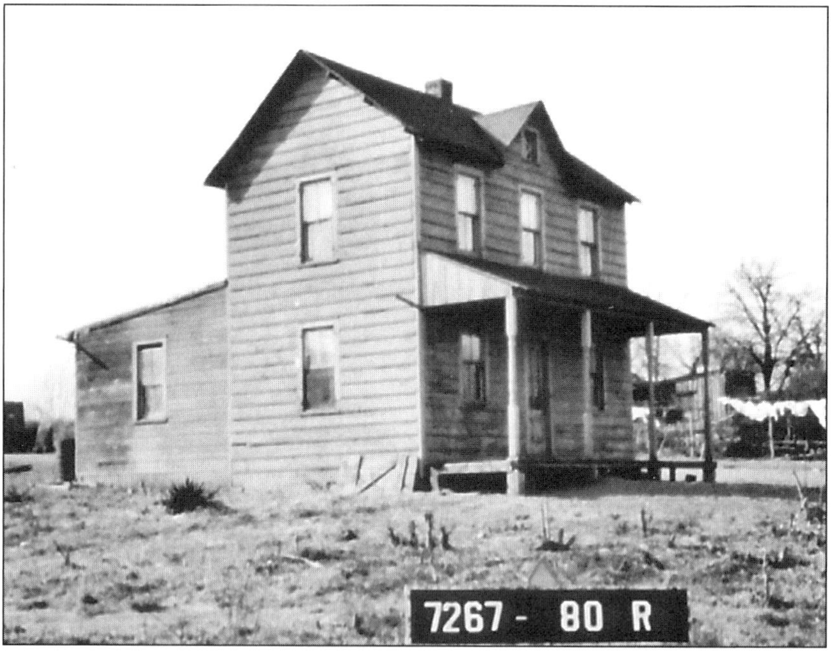
7267- 80 R

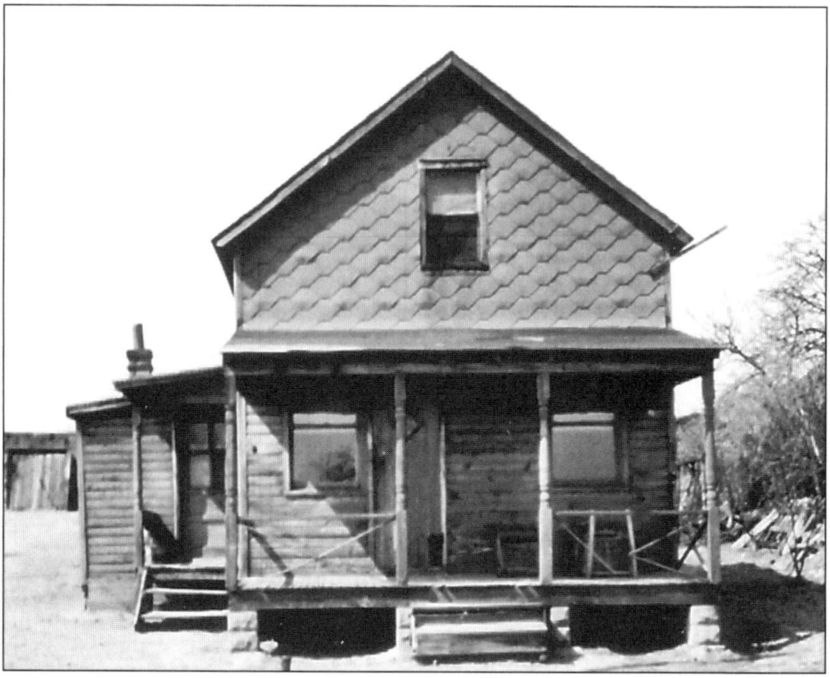

536 Bloomingdale Road

This frame house was probably built around 1900. In the 1940s it was owned by Rebecca Gray Landin, who held several Sandy Ground rental properties. Elmer and Octavia Decker, Isabelle Jones, Elmer Tate and others lived here at various times.

542 Bloomingdale Road

This house was probably built around 1910. In the 1940s William Bishop Jr. and his wife Naomi (William was a brother of Joseph Bishop, the blacksmith) lived here, as did Charles and Helen Logan, among others.

548 Bloomingdale Road

This Queen Anne-style house was built about 1890 for Francis and Mary Emily Henry, Lois Mosley's paternal grandparents. They resided here until the end of their lives. Lois lived here in the 1930s. Aunt Flora "Flossie" Henry made it into a "resort" in the 1950s. The house was heavily damaged in the fire of 1963 and not rebuilt.

552 Bloomingdale Road

Norma Wallen McGhie spent her earliest childhood in this house, terming it "the old house." It had been built by Robert and Rebecca Gray Landin, her maternal grandparents. "Uncle Jimmy's" house, 556 Bloomingdale Road, is on the right.

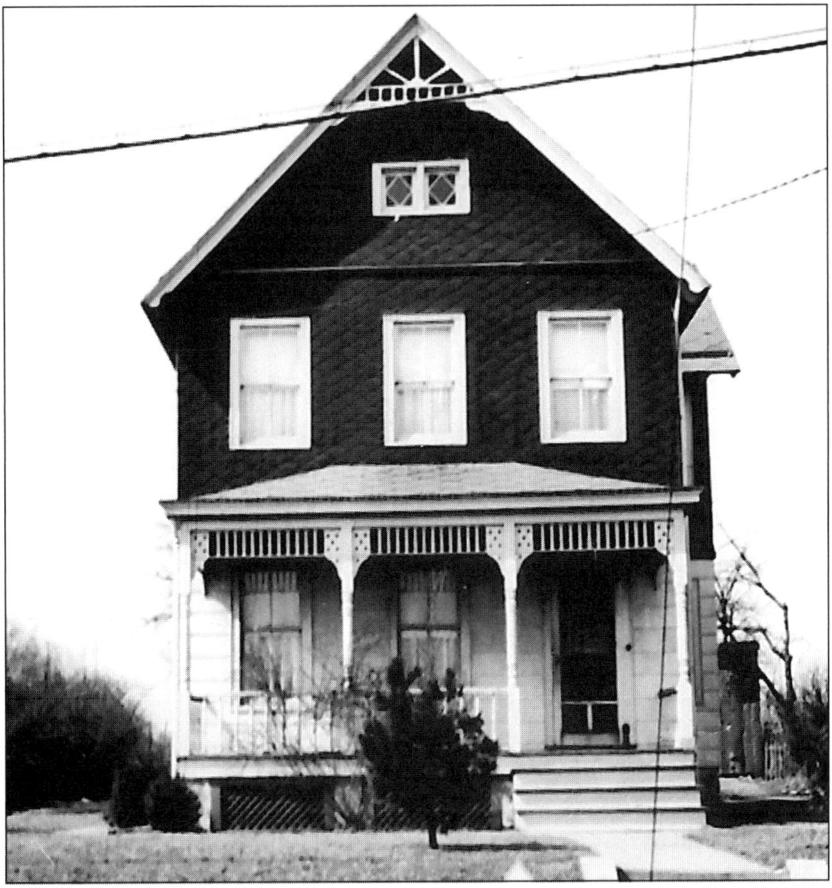

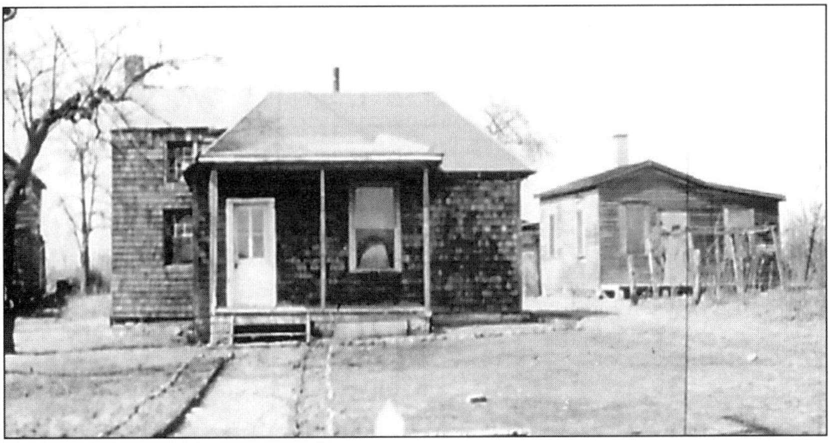

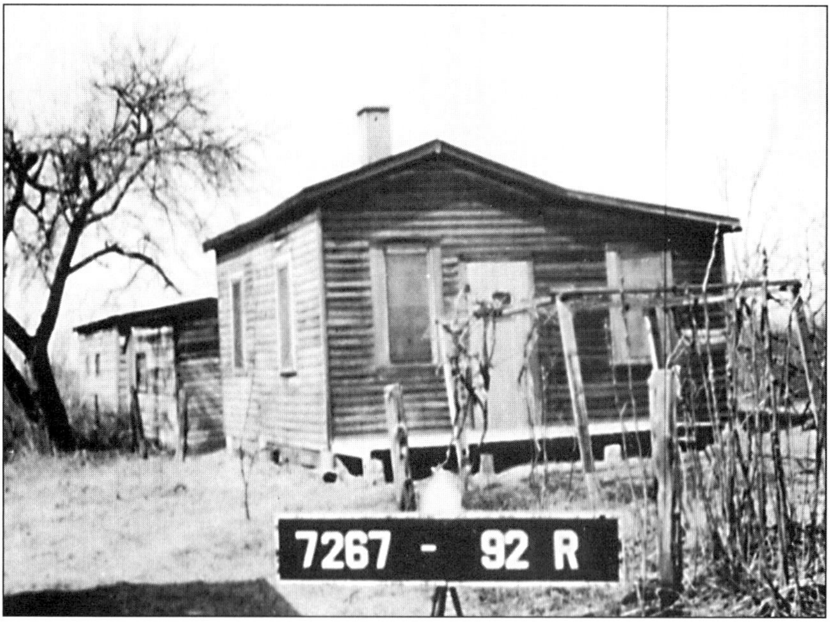
7267 - 92 R

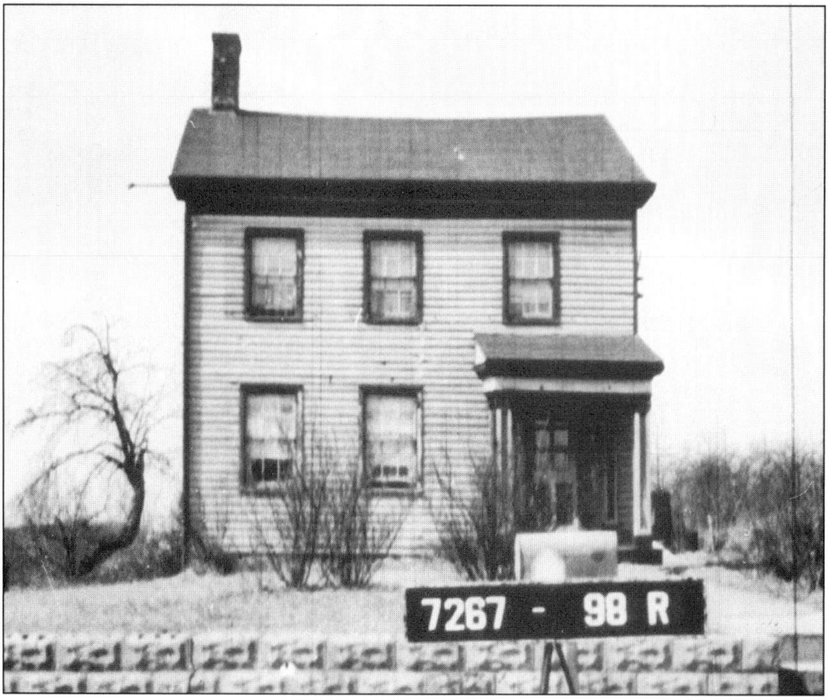
7267 - 98 R

556 Bloomingdale Road

This simple three-room frame house without a permanent foundation was probably built by the owner himself, James Decker ("Uncle Jimmy").

570 Bloomingdale Road

Built about 1870, this three-bay clapboard house was typical of Staten Island's 19th-century domestic architecture. The straight gable roof and end chimney likewise represent this tradition. Beers' 1874 atlas gives the owner's name as E. Napoleon, and Elizabeth Napoleon's name appears in Bromley's 1917 atlas. The 1875 Census lists Elizabeth as a black woman, born in Virginia, aged 56. Lois Mosley spent the first years of her childhood in this house. It was destroyed in the fire of 1963.

584 Bloomingdale Road, The Rossville A.M.E. Zion Church

Pictured here is the congregation's present (second) church building, which was first occupied on Dec. 19, 1897 (Hubbell's *History of Methodism and the Methodist Churches of Staten Island,* [1898], p. 149). The new building, in a prominent location, gave the congregation more visibility, but there were only 48 members. "It was largely due to the energy and perserverance of Homer [Omer] Harris that they were able to erect the new building." (Hubbell, p. 152.) Staten Island citizens outside the congregation contributed toward its $5,000 cost. The *Richmond County Advance*, Sept. 18, 1897, states that the new church was constructed by builder Andrew Abrams of Pleasant Plains.

The simple frame meetinghouse with straight gable roof and high basement has double paneled doors in the center and peaked cornices above the windows, its primary ornamentation.

The first church building had been erected after 1854 in what is today's Rossville A.M.E. Zion cemetery on Crabtree Avenue. This building was made of wood and seated 125 people (Hubbell, p. 149). It continued in use for some years after 1897 as a Sunday School and meeting hall. No image of it is known to have survived (except for its "footprint" in several atlases). The date of its demolition is not known.

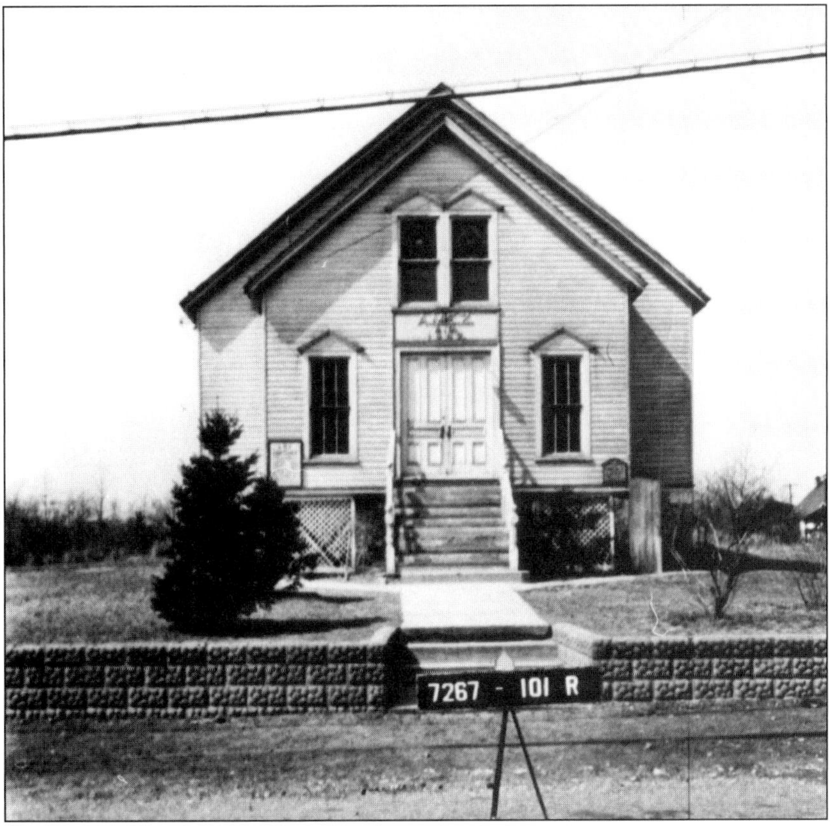
7267 - 101 R

Nineteenth Annual Camp Meeting

Broadside, 18 x 12 in., 1908. Collection of Lois Mosley. This poster lists speakers and dates of meetings. It provides several portraits and a view of the church building.

| 1853 | Nineteenth Annual | 1908 |

CAMP MEETING

OF THE

African Methodist Episcopal Zion Church

✍ WILL BE HELD ✍

RT. REV. GEO. W. CLINTON, A. M., D. D.
Presiding Bishop New Jersey District.

In the Tent at Westfield on Bloomingdale Ave.,

Between Pleasant Plains and Rossville, S. I.

Near Pleasant Plains R. R. Station.

Come and consecrate yourselves to the Lord and receive His blessings.

Our Tabernacle Meeting Begins Saturday evening, Aug. 1, 1908

Praise Meeting at 7 p. m. led by Rev. Robert Landin. Preaching at 8 p. m.

RT. REV. A. WALTERS, A. M., D. D.
Ex-Presiding Bishop New Jersey District.

Sun. Aug. 2

will be the

Great Gathering

The bugle sound will be heard with the praises of God.

Sunday, Aug. 9

the battle cry will go forth within and without the camp.

A. M. E. ZION CHURCH

Sunday, Aug. 16

will be a high day in Zion with the daughters of Jerusalem coming up to the battle of the Lord.

Services will be held each evening during the week at 8 p. m. Each service will be followed with an invitation for souls to join the army of the Lord.

REV. JAS. S. DECKER,
Richmond Valley.

Prominent among the visitors who will sound the alarm :

Rt. Rev. Geo. W. Clinton, A. M., D.D., Charlotte, N. C ; Rt. Rev. A. Walters, A. M., D. D., New York; Dr. John F. Moreland, Charlotte, N. C.; Dr. W. H. Coffee, Phila.; Dr. C. D. Hazel, P. E., Altantic City; Rev. R. R. Ball, D. D., Jersey City; Rev. J. J. Adams, D. D.; Rev. J. B. J. Rhodes; Rev. E. M. Compton, Rev. W. D. Robeson; Rev. F. R. Walton; Rev. C. H. Brown; Dr. W. T. Biddle, Rev. A. P. Miller, D. D.; Prof. J. W. McDonald; Rev. D. E. Land, B. D.; Rev. J. H. Hudgins; Rev. S. Marks; Rev. Jas. S. Decker; Rev. Robt. Landin; Dr. Thos. H. Amos, Paterson, N. J.; Rev. Mrs. Anne Smith, Norristown, Pa.; Rev. Mrs. Martha Ivins, Asbury Park; Rev. L. Roach and Rev. V. Linsey.

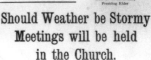

DR. C. D. HAZEL,
Presiding Elder

All are Cordially Invited

Remember the Date

Musical Dept.

The very best talent will be selected to gladden the hearts of those present, under the direction of our chorister, Prof. Geo. E. Henmon, Miss Mamie Bishop, Organist, and others.

H. H. HARRIS, President.

JOEL COOLEY, Secretary.

For all information see circulars and programs or write the pastor, Rev. Jas. E. Sarjeant, P. O. Box 72, Prince Bay.

PROF. J. W. McDONALD,

Should Weather be Stormy Meetings will be held in the Church.

TRUSTEES

James McCoy, President; George Henry, Secretary; John Tylor, Treasurer; H. Harris, Geo. Henmon, Charles Moody, Wm. D. Landin. Preacher's Steward, Geo. Purnell. William D. Landin, Church Clerk. Rev. Jas. E. Sarjeant, Pastor.

Marshals, Mr. Jacob Finney, Mr. Stephen Davis.

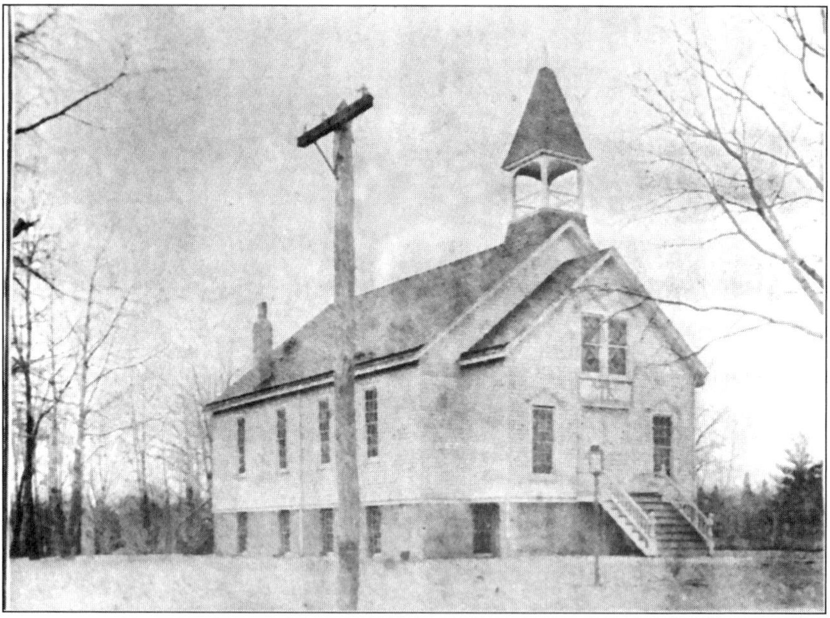

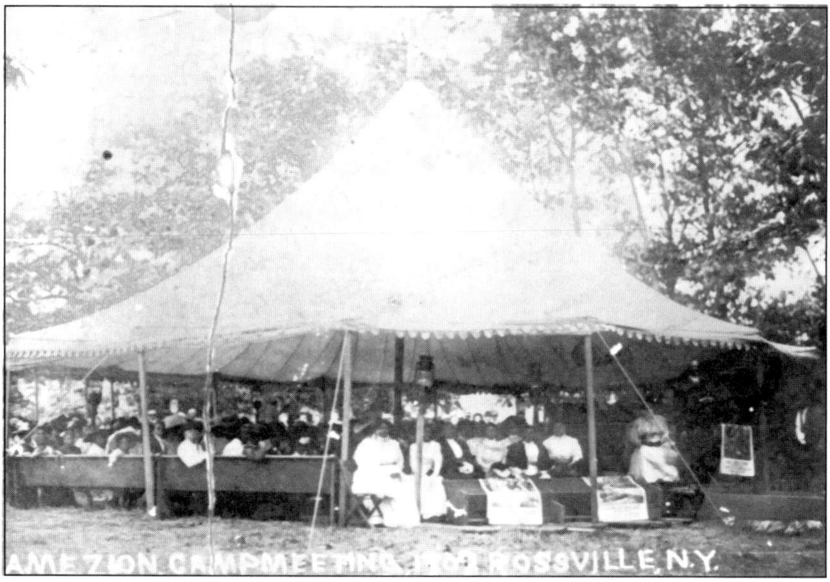
AME ZION CAMPMEETING
ROSSVILLE, N.Y.

Rossville A.M.E. Zion Church, 1908

This earliest known view of the church shows its bell tower. [Detail of broadside, page 175.]

A.M.E. Zion Camp Meeting, Rossville, N.Y., 1902

Postcard: Lois Mosley's collection. Participants pose for the camera in the camp meeting tent. Camp meetings were annual summer events for decades. They attracted crowds of both African American and white enthusiasts.

"A.M.E. Zion, Campmeeting, 1909, Rossville, N.Y."

Postcard: Lois Mosley's collection.

Annual Carnival & Barbecue ticket, August 24, 1940

Lois Mosley's collection. Ox roasts and barbecues were popular fund-raisers for the Rossville A.M.E. Zion Church. Many people remember them today.

A.M.E. ZION CAMPMEETING 1909, ROSSVILLE N.Y.

Annual Carnival & Barbecue

Will be given by

The A. M. E. ZION CHURCH

Bloomingdale Road, Pleasant Plains, S. I.

SATURDAY AFTERNOON, AUGUST 24th, 1940

Under the auspices of the TRUSTEES

Geo. Hunter, President　　　　W. D. Laudin, Treasurer
A. Decker, Secretary　　　　J. B. Kirby, Pastor

SPORTS AT 4 O'CLOCK

DINNER　　[3 to 10 P. M.]　　50 CENTS

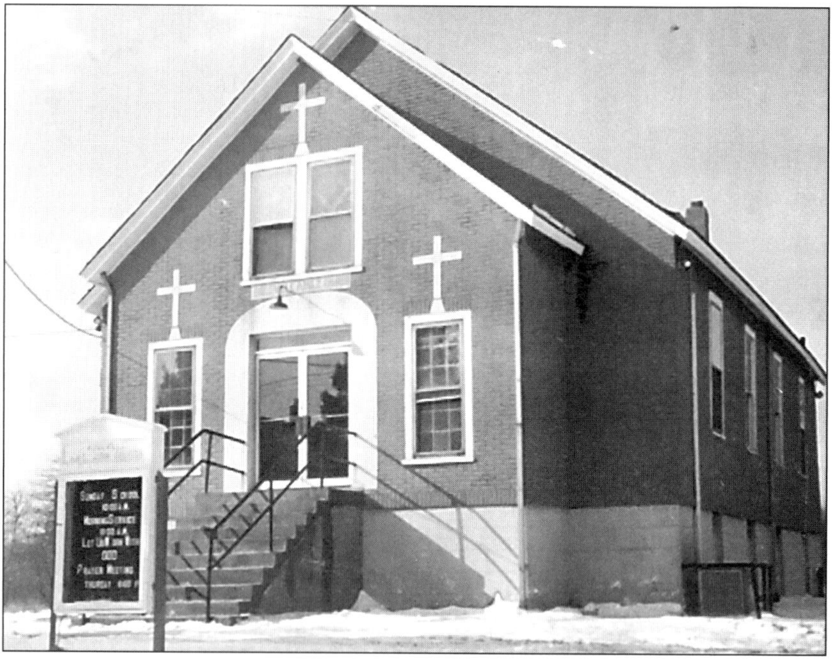

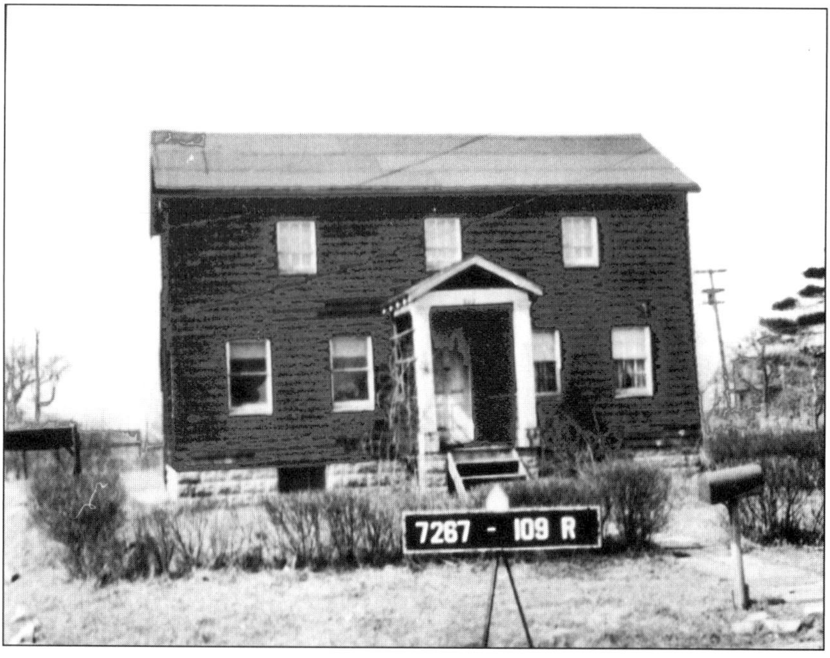
7267 - 109 R

The Rossville A.M.E. Zion Church, 1980

Photograph by Lois Mosley. This building is in use today.

592 Bloomingdale Road

This five-bay house stood to the right of the church. In Lois's youth it was the residence of the Bartlett family, who were white.

Wilburn's Gas Station. Bloomingdale Road, corner of Clay Pit Road

Mailboxes for the residents of Clay Pit Road stand in a row alongside the gas station near the intersection. 610 Bloomingdale Road is in the background.

610 Bloomingdale Road

This residence was probably built ca. 1875. Its wraparound porch has gothic cutwork trim above elegant posts. The double doors, pointed gothic attic window, and bracketed eaves are impressive.

Charles Bogardus, a white man, may have been the original owner. His name appears on the property in Beers' atlas, 1887; Sanborn's atlas, 1898; and E. Robinson's atlas, 1907. According to Lois Mosley it was owned by the Wilburn family in the 1930s. They probably added the gas station. Millie Stout and her mother lived here, too. The Ware family, who came from New Brighton and were black, owned the house in the 1950s while a Mr. Williams ran the gas station.

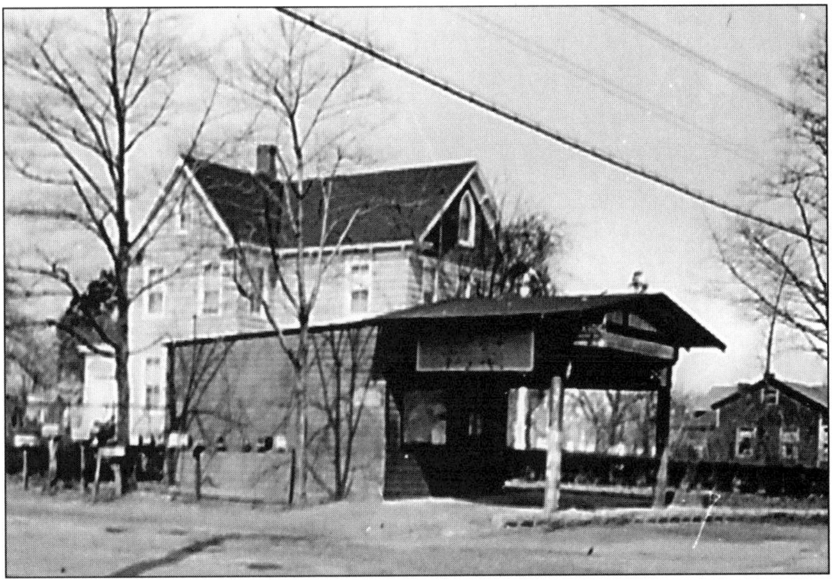

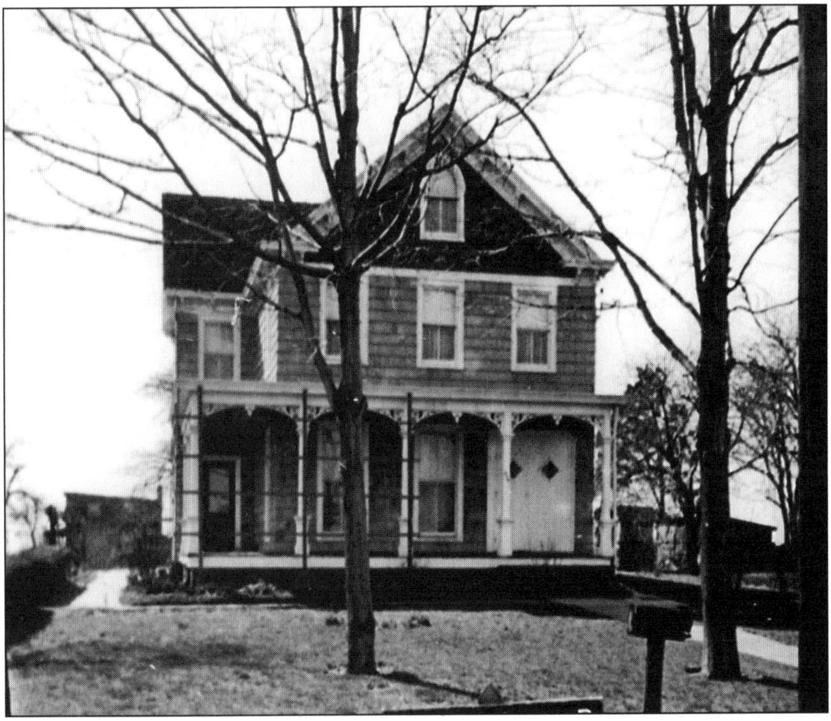

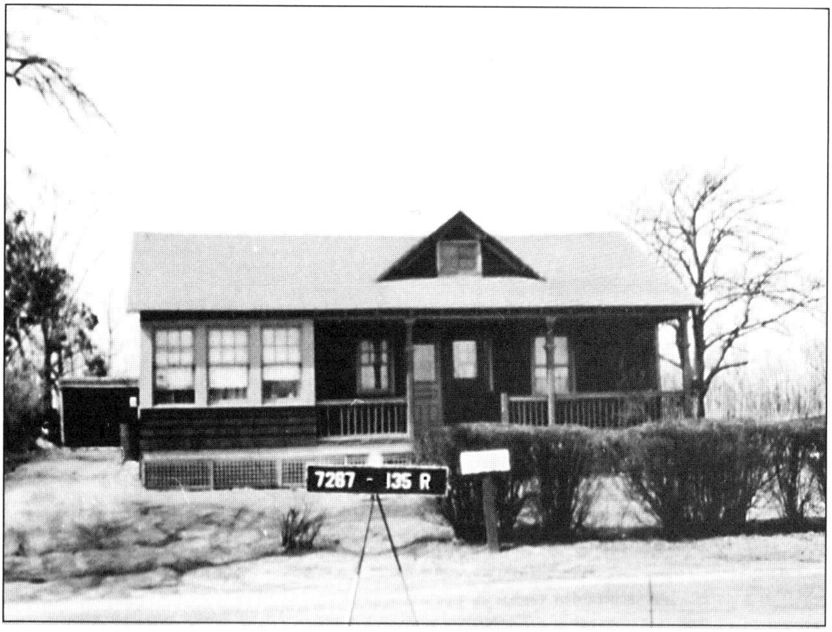
7267 - 135 R

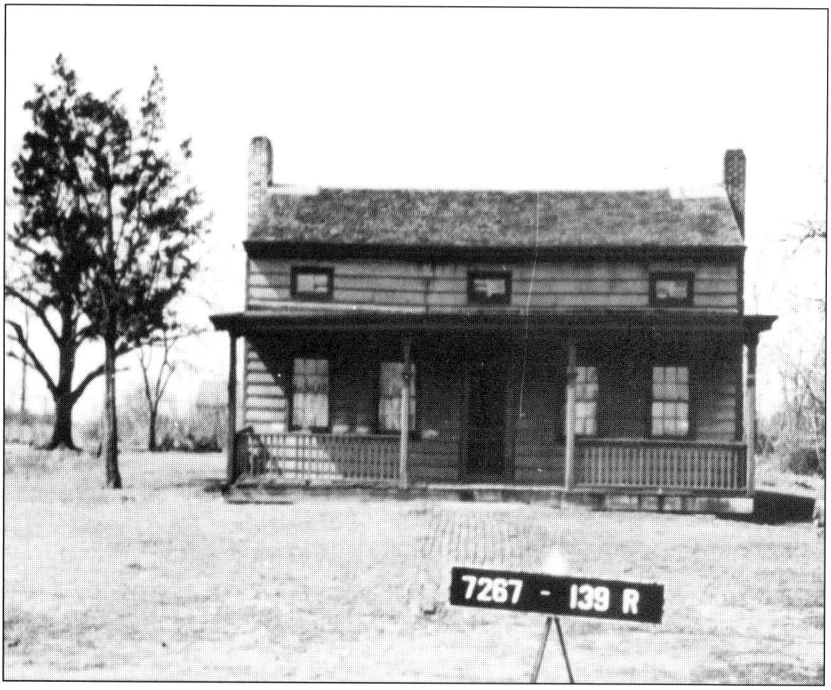
7267 - 139 R

624 Bloomingdale Road

Built for Omer Harris and his wife Josephine after 1896, when they acquired the land. They were Lois Mosley's maternal great-grandparents. This house was in the Bungalow style, unusually low in profile, not typical of Staten Island architecture of this time. Lois believes it was designed by members of the architectural firm of McKim, Mead and White, at the request of Omer's cousin, Isaac Harris, an employee in Stanford White's household.

The house was later occupied by Charles and Ethel Harris, Omer and Josephine's son and daughter-in-law. Charles was a construction worker. Charles's step-daughter Gladys Barringer resided in this house in the 1950s and 1960s. It was demolished in 1999.

640 Bloomingdale Road

This five-bay clapboard house was for many years the parsonage of the Rossville A.M.E. Zion Church. In the 1950s it was rented to Mae and Milford Moody.

P.S. 31, 650 Bloomingdale Road, corner of Crabtree Avenue

Photograph: New York City Board of Education Archives, Milbank Memorial Library, Teachers College, Columbia University. Built by the NYC Board of Education in 1904, this imposing two-room schoolhouse was named the Guyon School after the property's early owners, an old family of Huguenot descent. Architect Charles B. J. Snyder designed it. He worked for the Board of Education from 1891 to 1923 designing schools throughout the city. This was Sandy Ground's only brick building. Its high Dutch gables gave it distinction. Julia Hurd was principal in the 1930s when Lois Mosley attended.

P.S. 31 was closed in 1939 and the children dispersed to three different schools, P.S. 3 in Pleasant Plains, P.S. 6 in Rossville and P.S. 4 in Kreischerville. The Sandy Ground Historical Society, created in 1978, considered acquiring the building for their headquarters. It was subsequently acquired by a developer. In 1980 it was severely damaged by fire and demolished.

718 Bloomingdale Road

Home of Miss Sis. Earlier occupants included the Harpers. Today it is the residence of Lillian Sarjeant, daughter-in-law of Bishop James Sarjeant Sr.

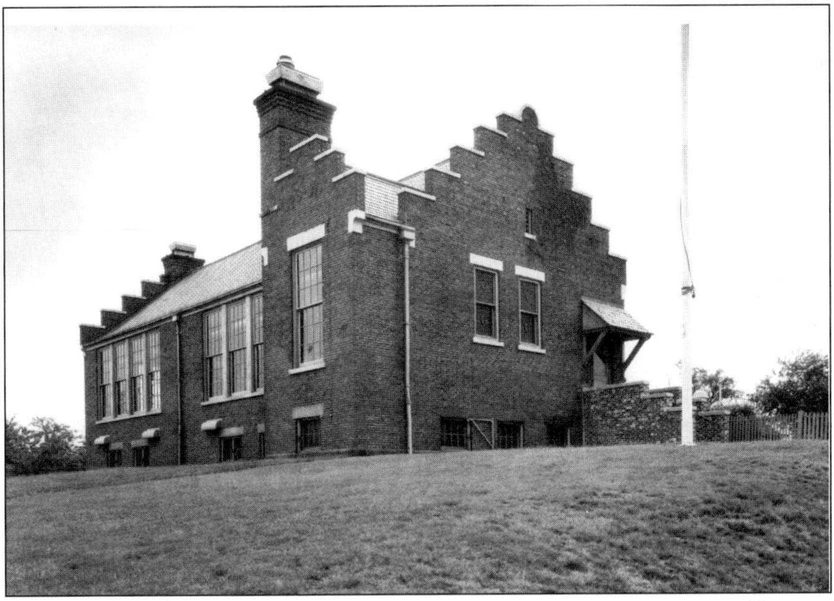

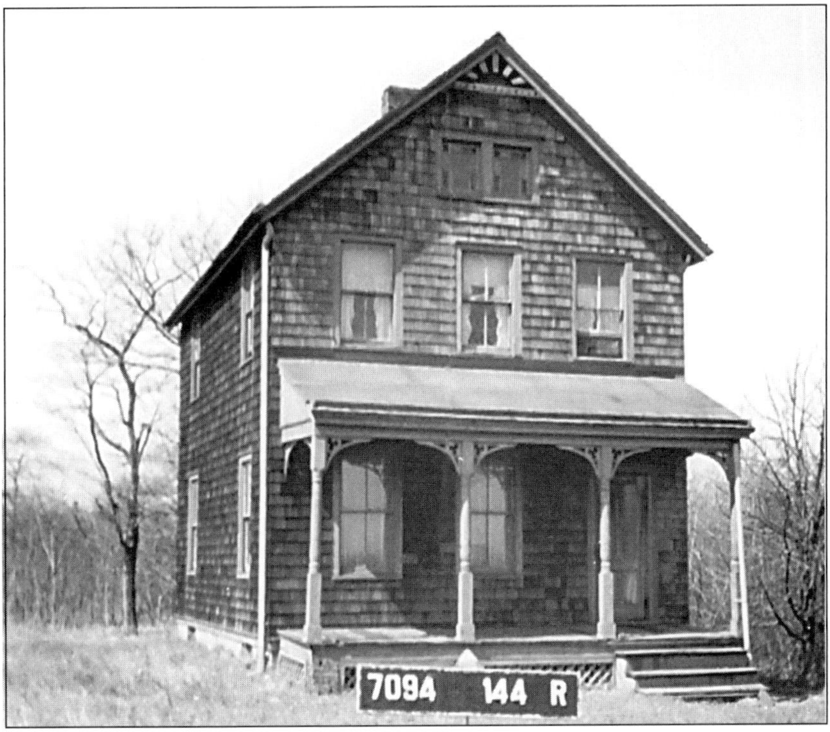
7094 144 R

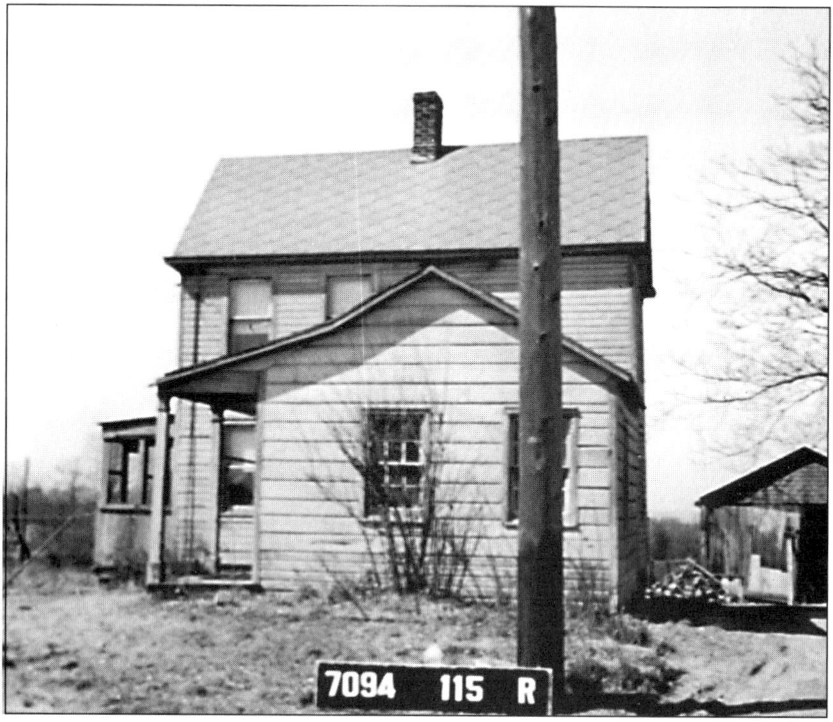
7094 115 R

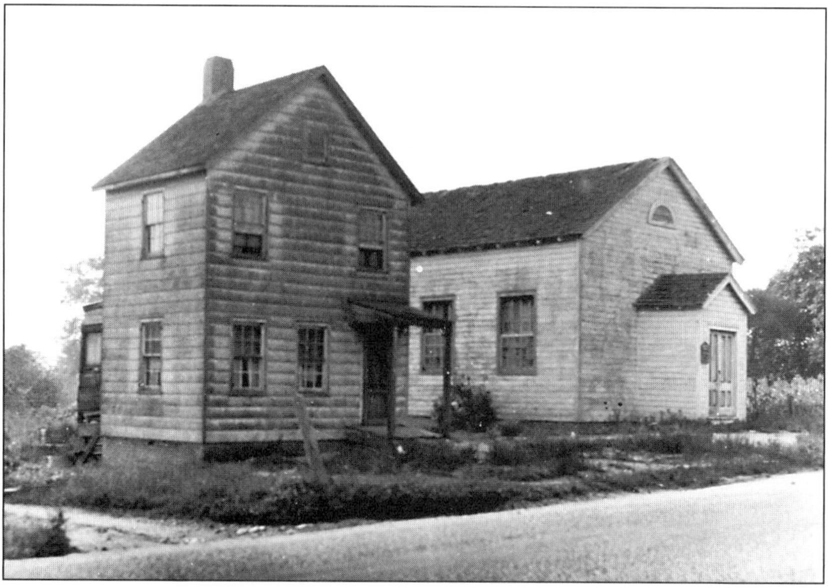

768 Bloomingdale Road

This simple two-story house with addition faces away from Bloomingdale Road. It was the home of Walter and Alice Henman and their daughter Geraldine who also lived here after her marriage to Hugh Enrick McDonald.

Mount Zion Methodist Episcopal Church and parsonage: Bloomingdale Road, number unknown

Photograph by Percy L. Sperr, Sept. 23, 1927. SIHS. The Mount Zion Church pictured here, along with the parsonage on the left, was founded in 1875 as an offshoot of the Rossville A.M.E. Zion Church down the street. According to Hubbell, G.M. Landin, the minister of the Rossville church, was asked by the congregation of the Port Richmond A.M.E. Zion Chapel to become their minister. He accepted the call, but without seeking the bishop's approval. When his action was reviewed by a committee appointed by the bishop and not sustained, he was unrepentant, and expelled from the church. The Rev. Landin then persuaded 57 Rossville parishoners to follow him into creating a new congregation, leaving only 13 members behind in the old church. The

Mount Zion Church, which they founded, joined the Newark Conference of the Methodist Episcopal Church (a predominantly white denomination).

The simple clapboard building was erected ca. 1880 and the parsonage ca. 1890. The formative years of the church were prosperous, as the new congregation was composed of Sandy Ground leaders who gave liberally. An account of a "Jubilee" held at the church appears in the *Richmond County Advance,* Jan. 11, 1896:

> There has been a Jubilee held by the Mt. Zion Sunday-School at Bogardus Corners, Westfield. This, of course, was for the children, and they were made very happy; but the older people wanted something to be jolly over also, and so they followed the Jubilee with an old fashioned Cake Walk, such as some of them had known down South. It was a time of excitement, and the contestants perspired and their friends shouted, and the meeting-house shook and trembled, and the Bible seemed inclined to jump from the pulpit, and the stove-pipe lost its perpendicular, and the coal-shuttle danced a jig, and everything was as gay as the jolliest colored man or woman could wish. We do not know the name of the gentleman who got the cake. Now, don't you pious white folks roll up your eyes and hold up your hands in holy horror, and say, 'What a desecration this is — of God's house! What a shame for professedly Christian people to indulge in such practices!' Better keep still — say nothing — sweep your own doorways clean.

Mount Zion Church remained, however, a mission church, at times affiliated with Rossville's St. John's Methodist Church (white) and sharing ministers with other churches (Hampton, 1965, p. 7). In the 1930s the congregation apparently decided to merge back into the Rossville A.M.E. Zion Church. Today several Sandy Grounders say they remember a ceremony for closing the building. The congregation assembled in Mount Zion Church and carried all the Bibles and hymnals in a solemn parade on Bloomingdale Road.

Bloomingdale Road: East Side

535 Bloomingdale Road

Photograph by Percy L. Sperr, June 1, 1930. Milstein Division of United States History, Local History & Genealogy, The New York Public Library, Astor, Lenox and Tilden Foundations. 1207 El. Grandma Cooper's house, 559 Bloomingdale Road, is seen on the left side of this picture. This early 19th-century farmhouse was built before the African American Sandy Ground community came into being. The older part, on the left, has small second-floor windows and its eaves have a shallow overhang. These features suggest a date of about 1830 or 1840. The two-bay wing on the right was added later, as was the porch. The 1850 maps indicate that it was owned by Mrs. J. Lee. Atlases of 1887 and 1898 show W. H. Hinds as the owner.

Oscar Prasse, a German immigrant, moved to Sandy Ground in 1912 to occupy this 12-acre farm. His son, Freeman Prasse, came with him as a child and kept on farming after his father's death. In the beginning they

grew mainly tomatoes, which they carried to Washington Market in Manhattan every day. In later years they grew strawberries and watermelons. After 1933 they began selling goat's milk. Soon they had a herd of 50 Nubian goats and their farm was the only certified goat dairy in New York City. Freeman Prasse remembered when strawberries were a big crop in Sandy Ground. He attended the ox roasts at the A.M.E. Zion Church. (Source: Joseph Mitchell interview, 1955. See also Meyer Berger, "About New York," ca. 1940, unidentified clipping, SIHS.)

559 Bloomingdale Road

Home of Sadie Roach Cooper ("Grandma Cooper"), who also ran a small grocery store here. Earlier a Mr. Rice lived here.

565 *(right)* and 569 Bloomingdale Road

These two cottages and a third in the rear (not visible) were built about 1900 by a white Staten Islander for rental as "baymen's cottages." During the 1940s the Moore family lived in No. 565 with their four children and later the Butlers, Thelma "Nan" Pedro, and John Turner.

No. 569 was occupied by a succession of families: William Landin and his daughter Beatrice Bevans; Geraldine and Hugh McDonald; Susan Henry (Lois Mosley's mother) and her children; Mrs. Turner; and Kenny Cooper, who still lives here.

These two houses still stand, the least modified old Sandy Ground buildings surviving on Bloomingdale Road. Susan Henry, Lois's mother, and her children lived in 569r Bloomingdale Road before moving into No. 569.

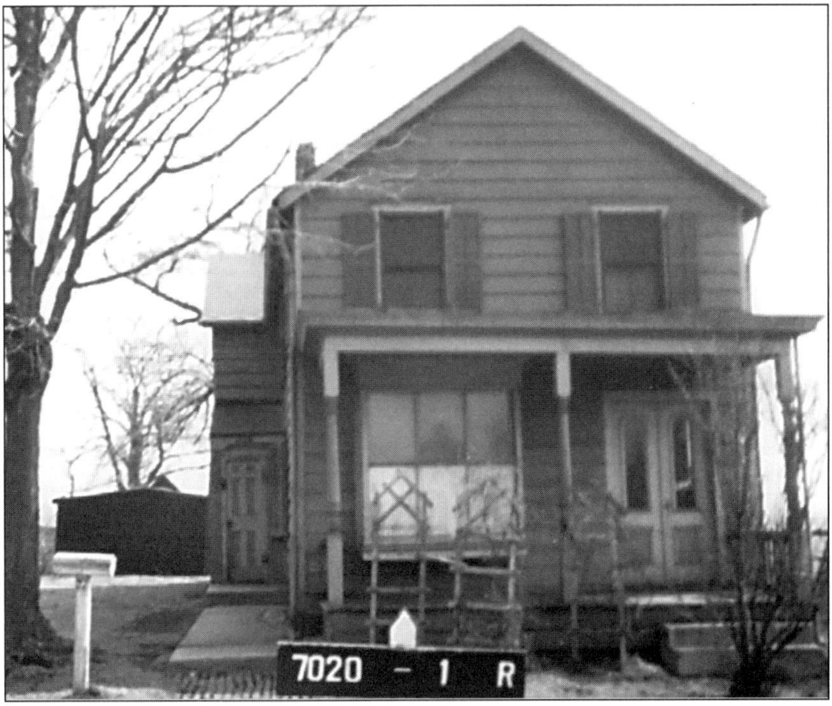
7020 - 1 R

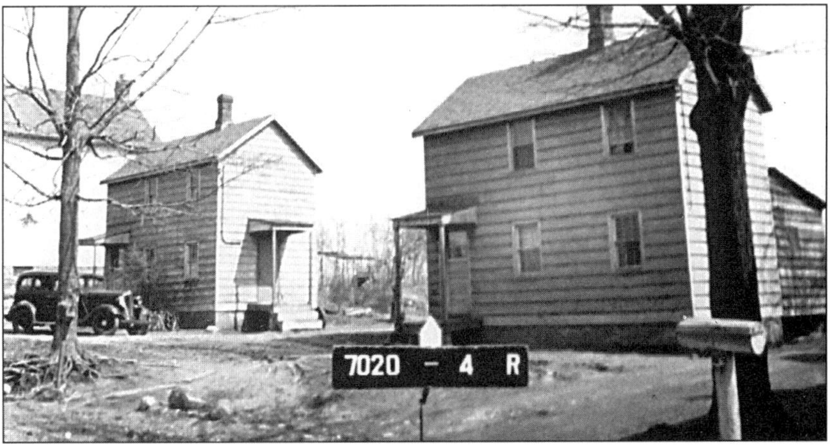
7020 - 4 R

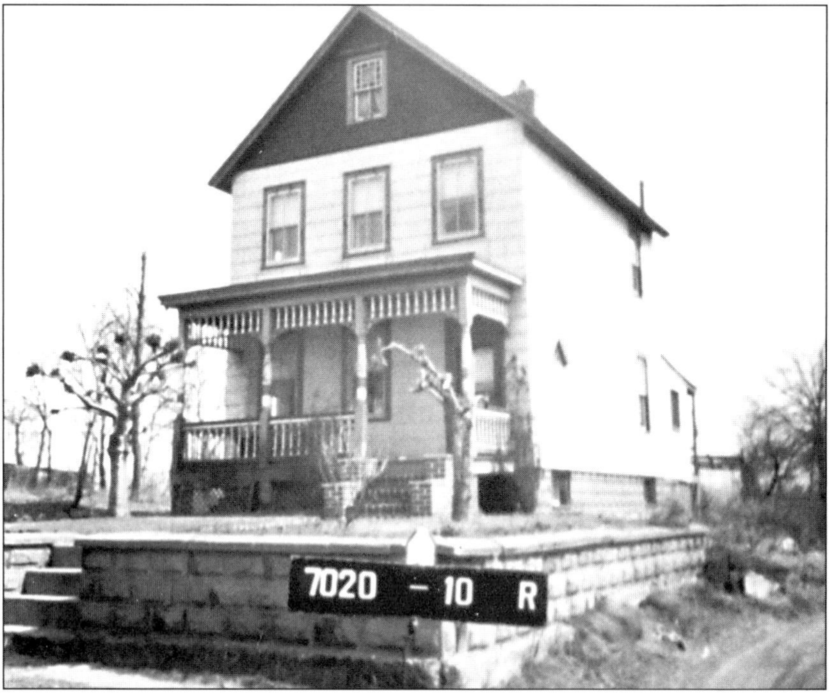
7020 - 10 R

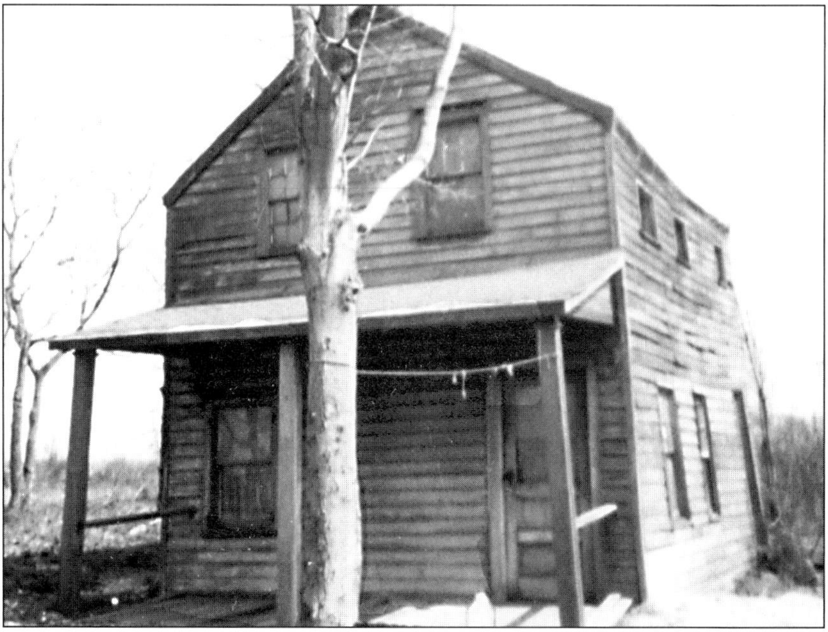

575 Bloomingdale Road, Mr. Hunter's House

This is the home of George H. Hunter, "Mr. Hunter" of Joseph Mitchell's *New Yorker* article, who lived here with his first wife, Celia, and then with his second wife, Edith. The house was probably built after 1906, when the Hunters bought the lot for $1 from Mr. Hunter's father-in-law. Its attractive turned porch posts and other decorative features were seen on many Staten Island houses. It still stands, much altered.

Mr. Hunter was the owner's representative for No. 565, No. 569, and No. 569r next door.

577 Bloomingdale Road

This was known as the Finney house. It stood back a distance from the road. In this photograph it leans to the left.

587 Bloomingdale Road

John Tyler Sr., who was born in Virginia, was an oysterman. He built this house in 1883, at the peak of Sandy Ground's prosperity. It became the home of William Harris (Mr. Wee), who married John Tyler's daughter.

Frances Henry Joseph, Lois Mosley's sister, lived here. Still later, William "Pop" Pedro and his daughter Thelma Pedro lived here. It was abandoned by 1993 and demolished in 1996.

591 Bloomingdale Road

This house was built in 1930 for Beatrice Bevans, who lived here with her father, "Uncle Billy" Landin. Aunt Helen Henry lived here later. Ralph Cooper purchased the house in the 1980s and it was demolished in the 1990s.

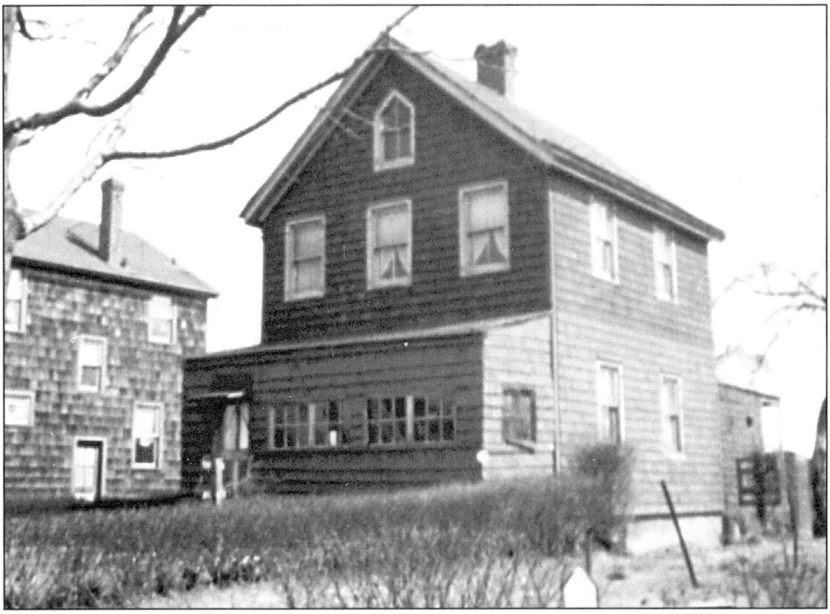

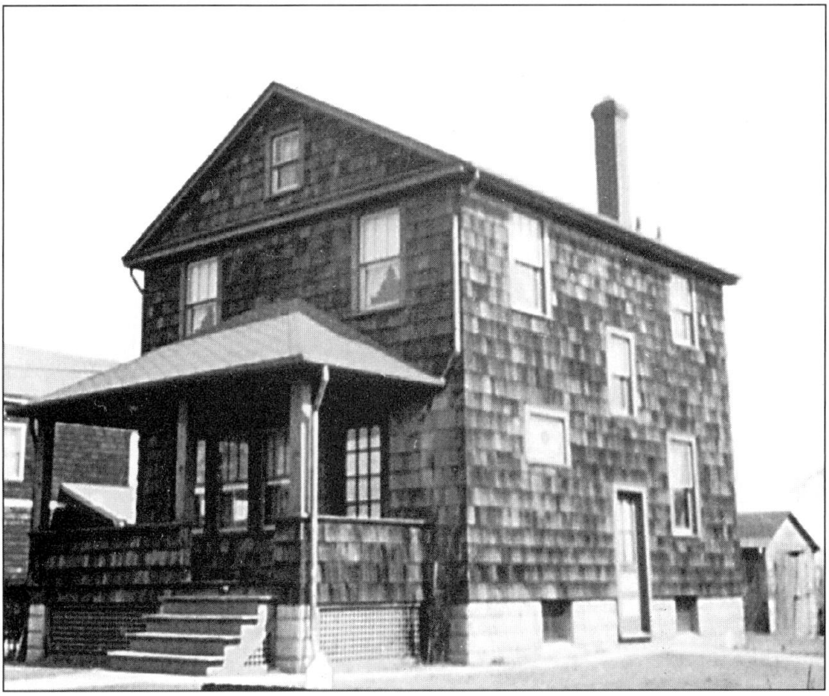

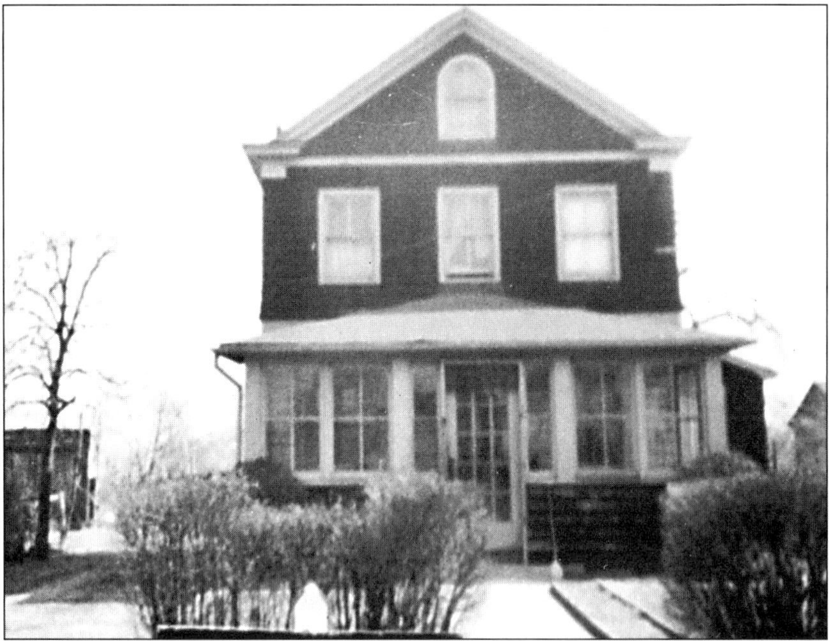

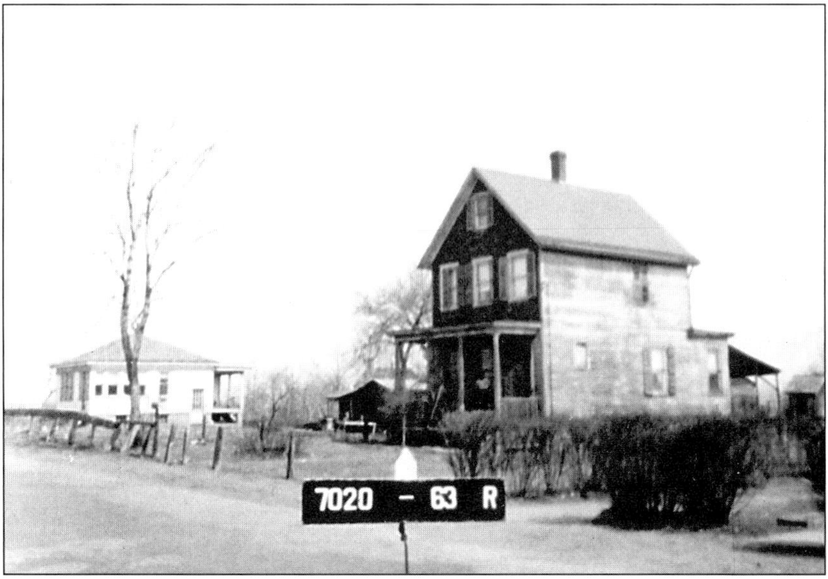
7020 - 63 R

599 Bloomingdale Road

This house, with its round-headed attic window and pronounced cornice, dates to the 1880s. The George Purnell family lived here in the 1880s and 1890s. Esther V. S. Purnell, George Purnell's wife, is said to be Sandy Ground's earliest teacher. Many other families lived here later, including Jim McCoy (who was a scoutmaster), Cora and Dennis Grady, Wally and Helen Koshick, and Julius Stovall. This house was was demolished in 1996.

605 *(right)* and 615 Bloomingdale Road

No. 605 was a three-bay house with gable end to the street. It once belonged to Charles Bogardus. During the 1930s and 1940s it was known as Mrs. Adeline Robinson's house. Adeline and her first husband, Mr. Miles, had two children, Hattie and Frank. The family came to live in Sandy Ground around 1913. Adeline's second husband, Mr. Robinson, commuted by small boat to his employment in a factory in New Jersey.

No. 615 was the home of Frank Miles, a carpenter who built it ca. 1920, living there into the early 1940s.

Rooming houses at Bogardus Corners, southeast corner of Bloomingdale Road and Woodrow Road

Photograph by William T. Davis, Sept. 30, 1934. SIIAS. Davis Collection 3620.4. These structures were built ca. 1900, probably by Charles Bogardus, for oyster workers and others. In the 1920s and 1930s they were owned by Rebecca Gray Landin. They were demolished before 1940.

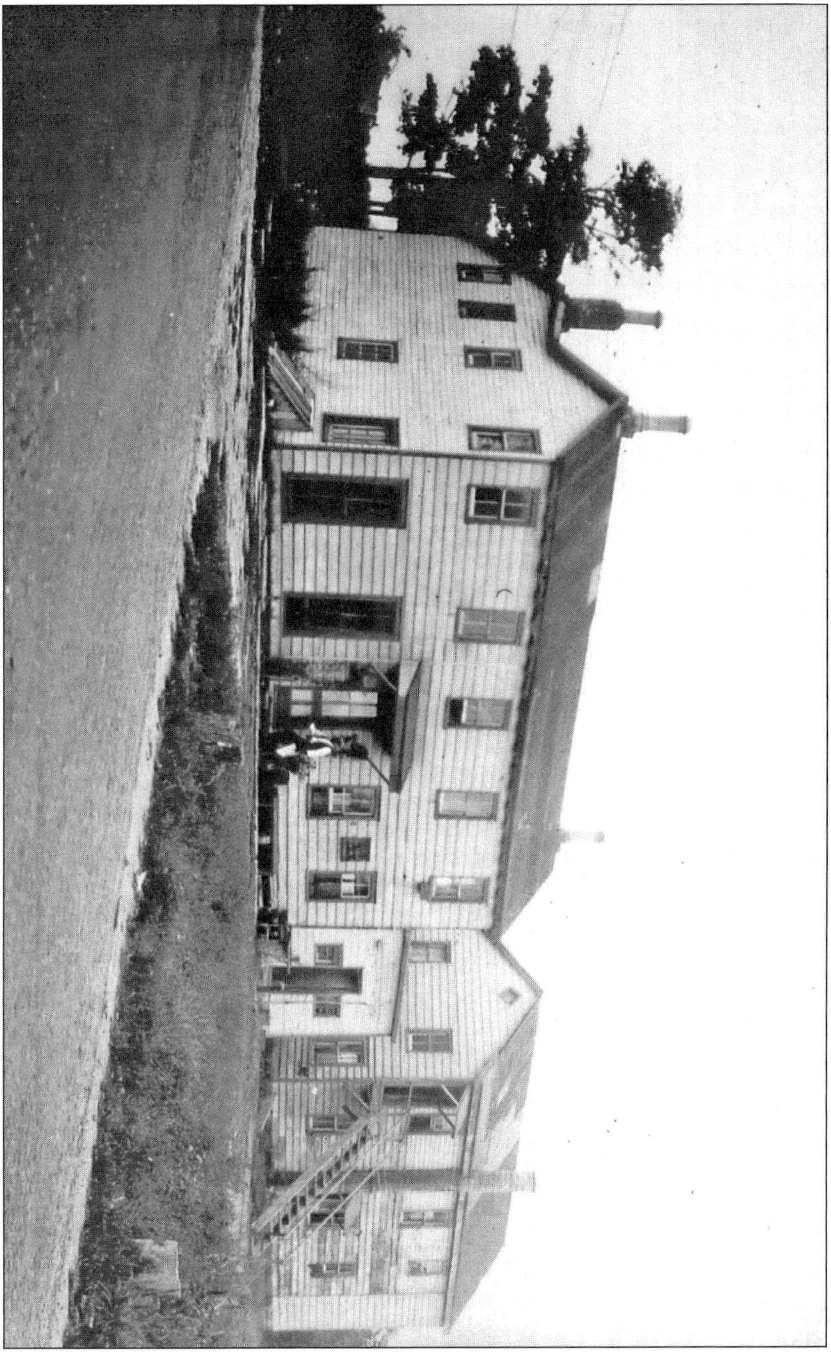

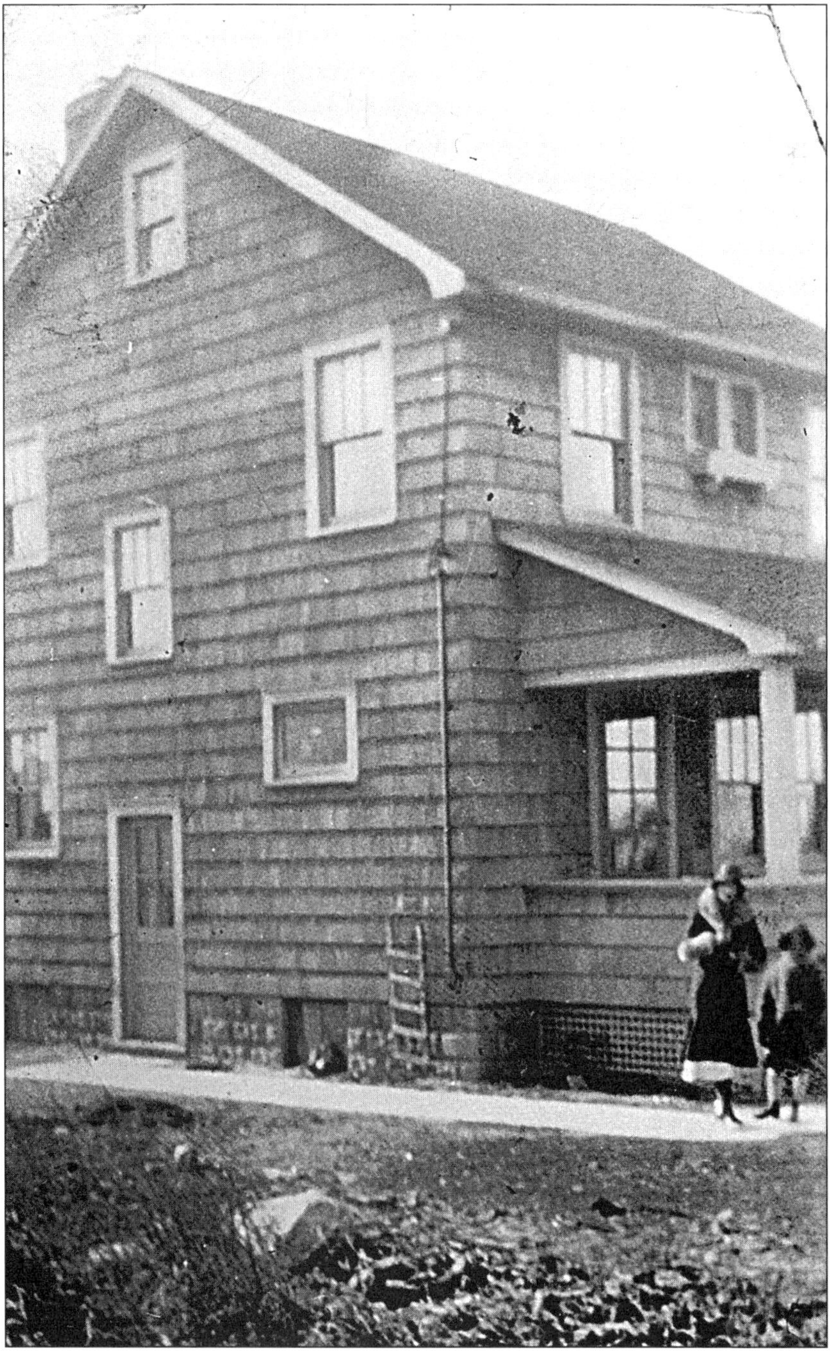

Clay Pit Road, South Side

26 Clay Pit Road

Photograph: Collection of Norma Wallen McGhie. In 1930 Alfred and Bertha Wallen built this house, the "new" house their daughter Norma writes about in this book. According to a Dept. of Buildings form, Mr. Wallen himself was the architect. The plans, which are still on file in the Dept. of Buildings, include living room, dining room, modern kitchen and three upstairs bedrooms. George Robinson of Tottenville was the builder. He also built the Bevans house at 591 Bloomingdale Road.

Kenneth Landin, Lois Mosley's uncle, purchased this house when the Wallens moved to Manhattan. Lois and Glemby Mosley were married here on Dec. 7, 1951. This house is still standing.

36 Clay Pit Road, The Pedro-Herring House

Photograph: Collection of Lucille Herring. This attractive house in the Bungalow style was built in 1923 by William "Pop" Pedro and his wife Susan Jane Bishop Pedro. It was designed and constructed by P. H. Nilsen of Richmond Valley, Staten Island. Mr. Pedro was a truck driver and chauffeur. Mrs. Pedro was a schoolteacher.

Their daughter, Hazel Elizabeth Pedro Herring, lived here after her marriage to Cleary Herring (from North Carolina). Today their daughter, Theresa A. Herring, a registered nurse at Staten Island University Hospital, resides here. Lucille Herring, another daughter, lived here in her youth. Also an RN and an epidemiologist, she lives today in Mariners Harbor and is active in the Sandy Ground community. Their aunt, Thelma "Nan" Pedro, contributed a chapter to this book.

40 Clay Pit Road

SIIAS photograph, 1979. Mr. and Mrs. William Brown lived at 40 Clay Pit Road during Lois Mosley's childhood. Mr. Brown was a NYC Dept. of Sanitation employee. Lois writes, "Mrs. Brown was a nice lady, but we kids thought that she was strange, that her eyes were held open by rubber bands around her head. We couldn't have been too scared of her because we loved her cakes and goodies. When Mrs. Brown spoke she would spray you. She had a juicy mouth."

Like its twin, No. 36 next door, the house was designed by Peter H. Nilsen. When constructed in 1924, it was owned by the builder George Robinson.

Harold and Olive Moody, well-known Sandy Grounders who were married for over 50 years, lived here. Mrs. Moody was Olive Pedro, Pop Pedro's daughter. Today their children Eugene and Olivia Moody live here.

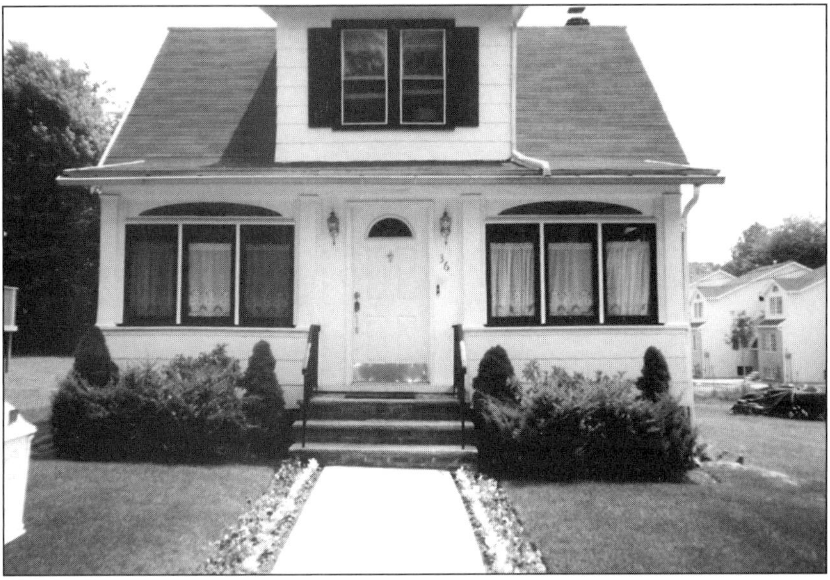

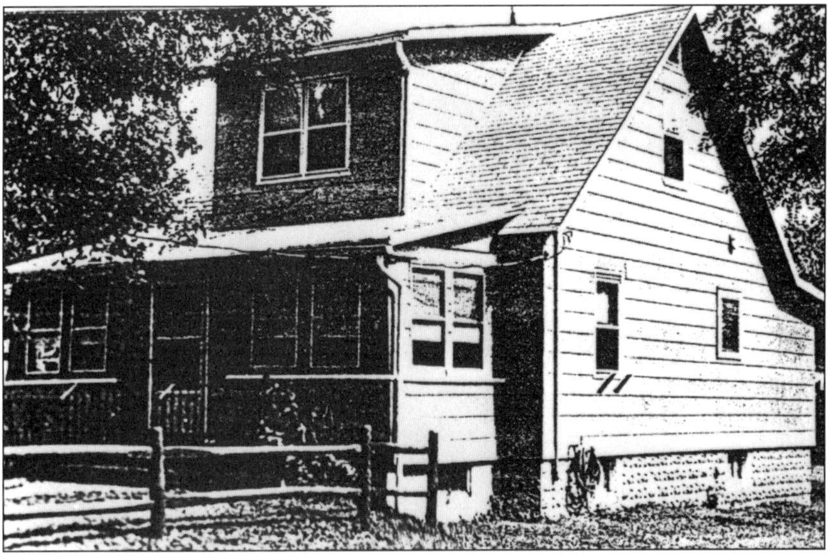

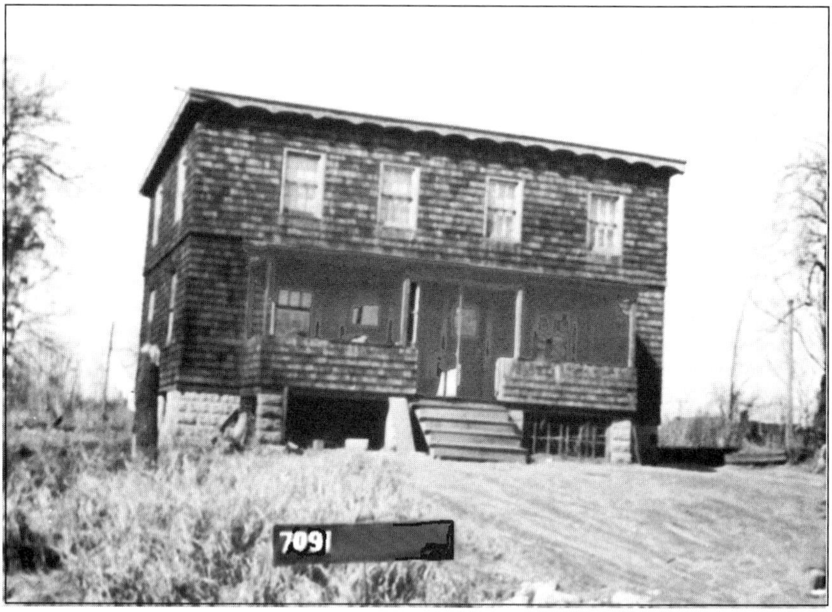
7091

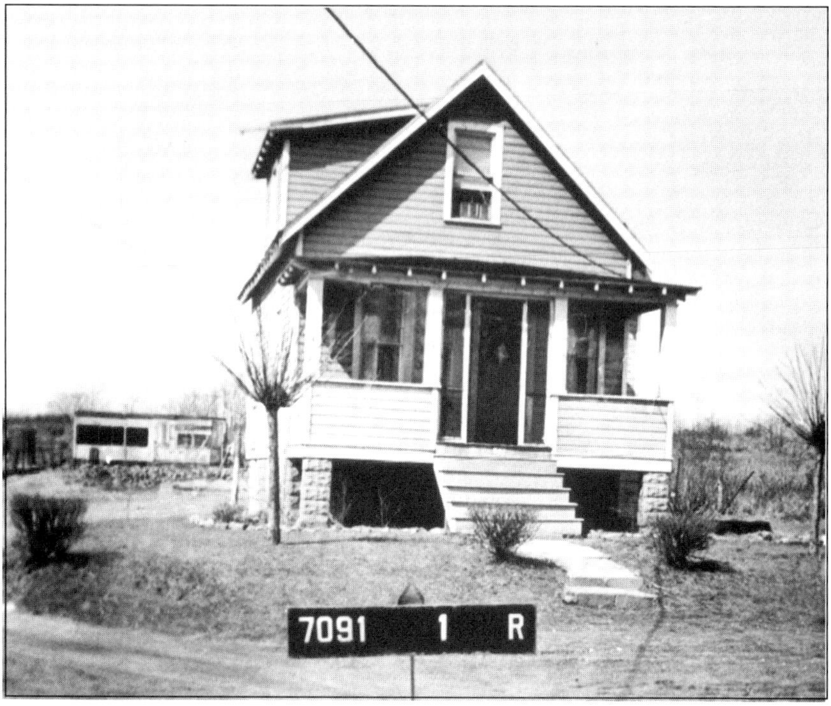
7091 1 R

Clay Pit Road, North Side

23-25 Clay Pit Road

Across from the Wallens was a large two-family brown house. It was originally owned by Charles Bogardus. Many Sandy Ground families rented this house including Gilbert (Tobe) Henman and Addie his wife; Harold and Olive Moody; Lillian and James Sarjeant; Beatrice Moore Brown; Calvin and Estherlina Moore; and Josephine and Lindwood Moore.

61 Clay Pit Road

This house was built for Fred Roach and his parents. It was rebuilt by John Cooper after the 1963 fire and Irene and Melvin Cooper lived here. In this photograph on the left is Fred Roach's chicken coop. It was here that the Sarjeants had their church services. Fred had tennis courts on the right side of the house.

Gilbert (Tobe) Henman and Addie Henman lived in a small house on the left side of this property (not in this photograph).

Harris Lane

Harris Lane, number unknown

Called by Lois Mosley "The Wood Peg House" or "The House Without Nails," this is thought to have been the home of Moses K. Harris and his brother Silas. They were among the pioneers of Sandy Ground, once known as "Harrisville."

The outward appearance of the house suggests a date of around 1850. The three-bay house with doorway is probably the original part, the two-bay part on the right being an addition.

William "Pop" Pedro said this house was his birthplace (Askins, 1980). Lois Mosley remembers it as the house of Mae Harris. She was the niece of Ike Harris and worked as a live-in maid at a Great Kills funeral parlor.

Harris Lane, number unknown

Photograph: Lois Mosley's collection, 1993. Here the house is abandoned and overgrown by trees. The large timbers joined by mortise and tenon can be seen.

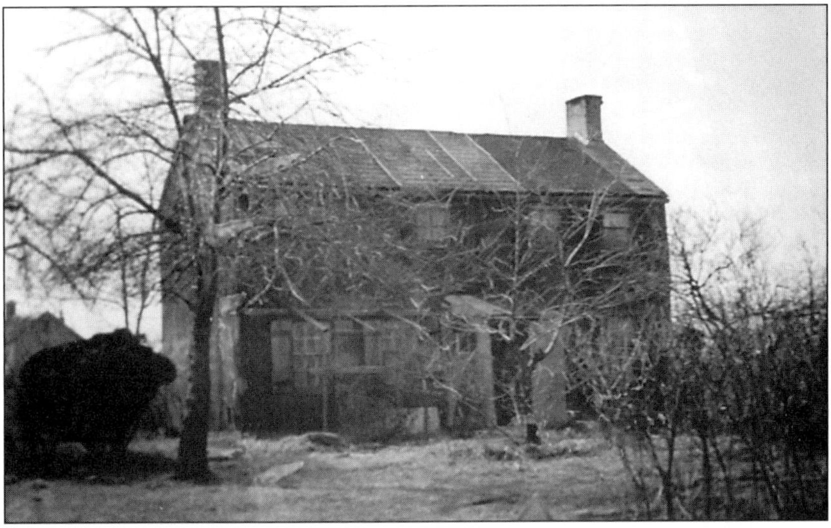

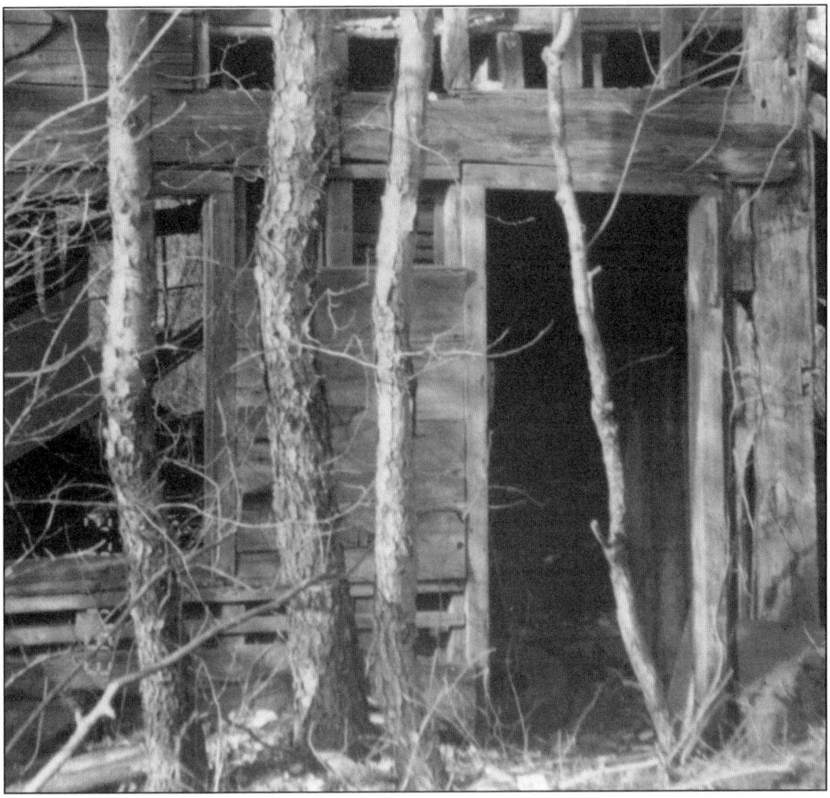

15 Harris Lane

SIIAS photograph, 1979. James Sarjeant Sr., a contemporary of Lois Mosley's father, lived here with his family. In his youth he was a boxer. Later he had a business cleaning cesspools (like Mr. Hunter). He left the Rossville A.M.E. Zion Church to found a holiness congregation at Sandy Ground. It became the Church of God in Christ, today located in New Brighton. In its early days the new church met in the former chicken coop behind Fred Roach's house at 61 Clay Pit Road. Mr. Sarjeant became a bishop in the denomination.

Norman Street—Down in the Woods

Water Street was an earlier name for Norman Street.

7 Norman Street

Naomi and Bill Bishop, of the "Good Time Crowd," lived here. Bill, who worked at the Nassau Smelting Refinery in Richmond Valley, was a brother of Joseph Bishop, the blacksmith.

23, 25 and 27 Norman Street

No. 23 (right) was the home of Malvina Moody Temple and her husband, Charles Temple, a construction worker. She wrote "My Life and Family" in this book.

No. 25 (middle) was the home of the Robert Washington family, which included five children. Mr. Washington worked at National Lead in Perth Amboy, N.J. This house was later lived in by Marian Sams and her three chidren.

No. 27 (partly visible, left) was home to the Smardels, a white family, and also Theodore Daniels, Carmilla Daniels' father. Later, Charles Temple and Malvina Moody Temple lived here.

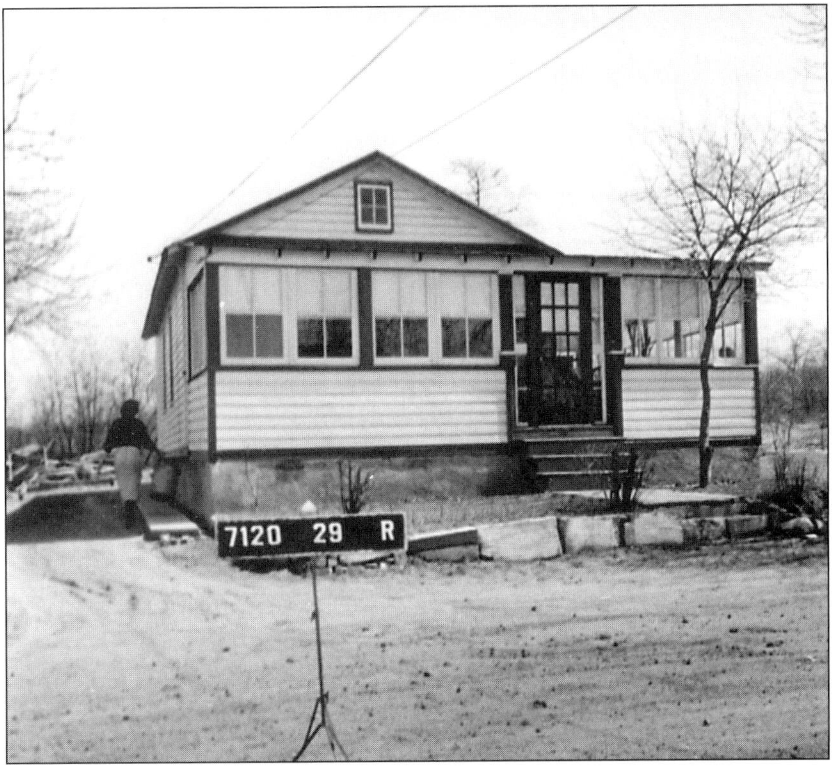
7120 29 R

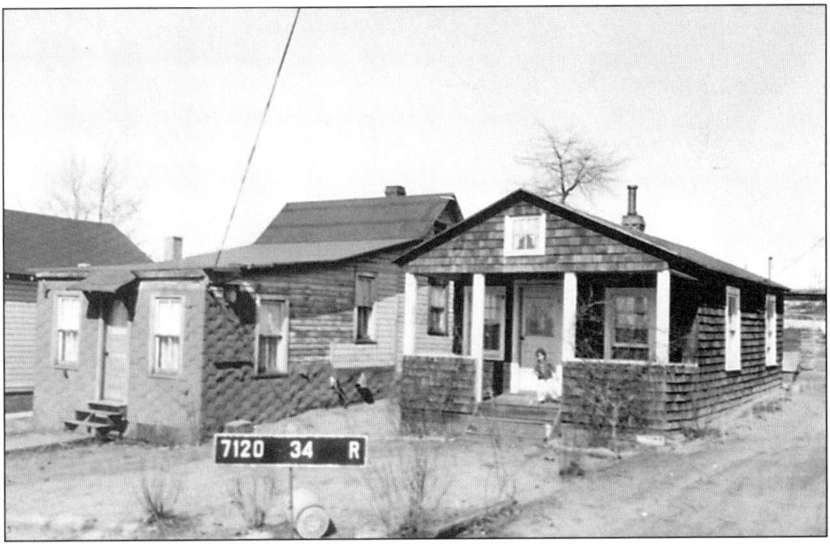
7120 34 R

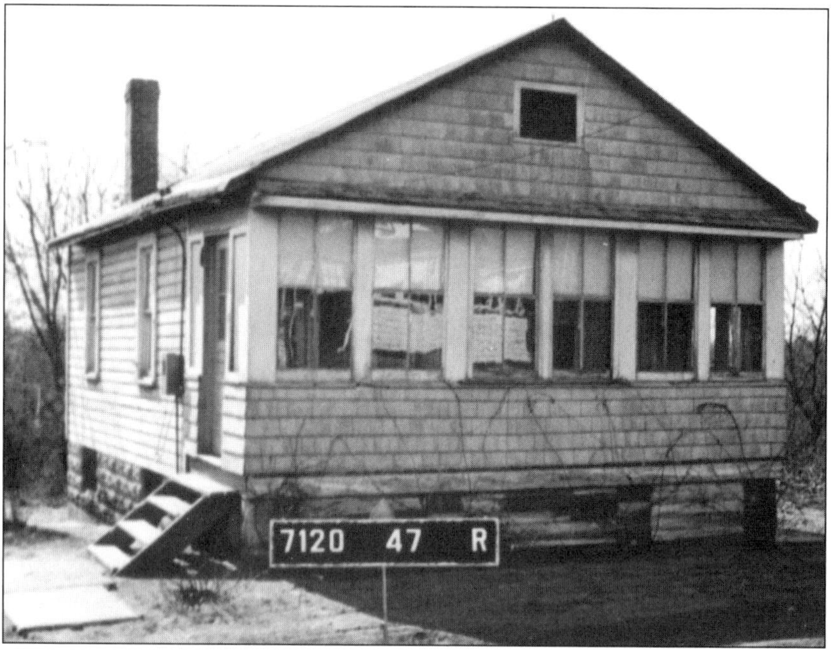
7120 47 R

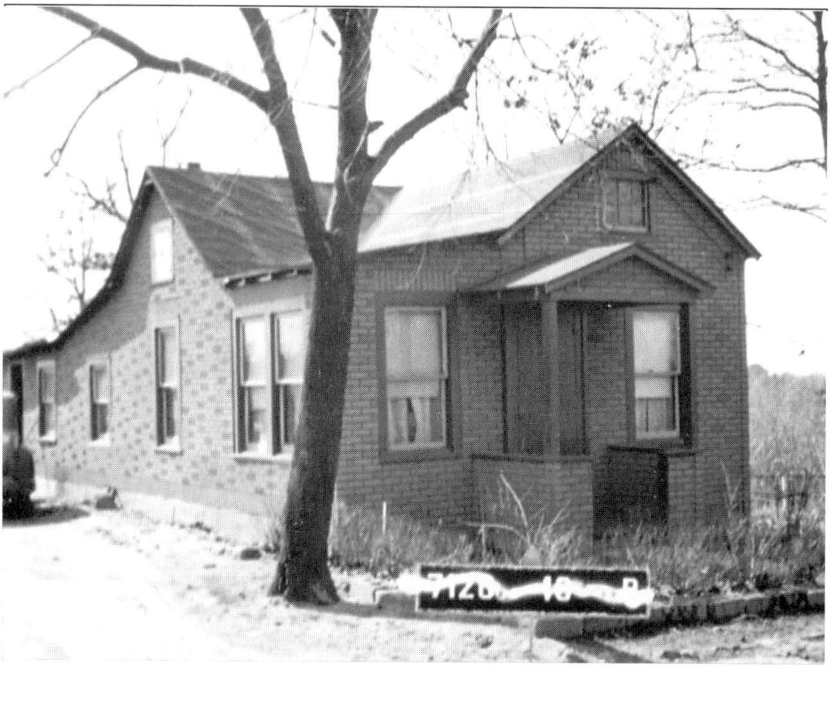

12 Norman Street

This was the home of the Eastmans. Mr. Eastman's nickname was "Coffee Cola." Jim Doby and Capt. Sanders boarded with the Eastmans.

14 Norman Sttreet

Marcellus Williams and family lived here. In the 1940s after the house burned they lived in the garage.

32 Norman Street

This was the home of Mr. and Mrs. Mangin. Later it was the home of James (Slim) Heard, who kept pigs and goats and had a smokehouse. He was known for his barbecues.

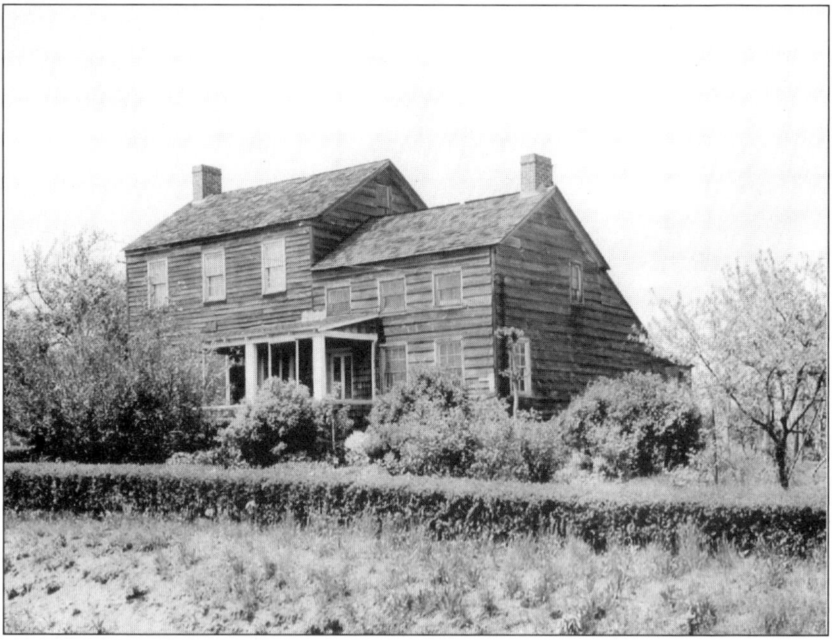

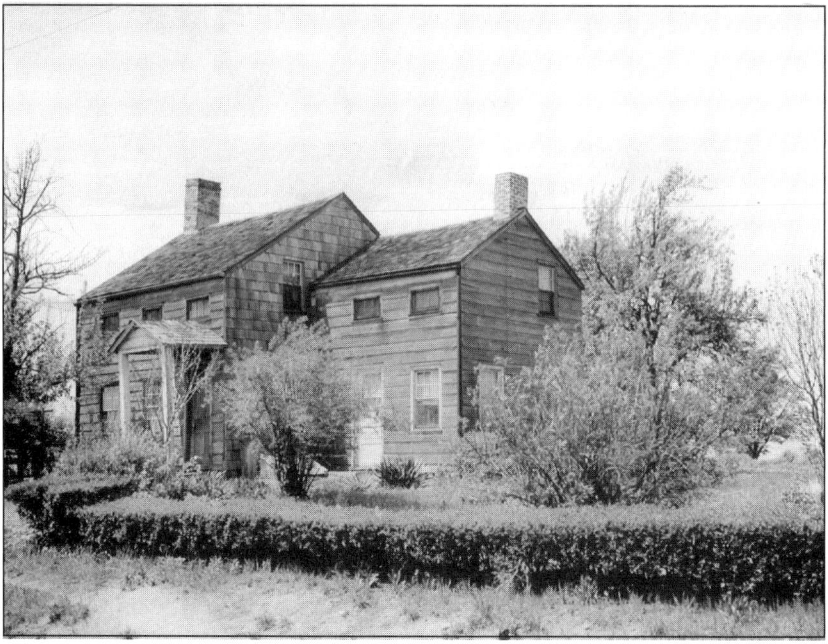

Sharrott's Road

183 Sharrott's Road

Photograph by Percy L. Sperr, May 12, 1937. Milstein Division of United States History, Local History & Genealogy, The New York Public Library, Astor, Lenox and Tilden Foundations. 1253 B5. This classic Staten Island farmhouse with straight gable roofs and end chimneys was probably built before 1850 by the Winant family: E. Winant's name appears on Butler's map of 1853. The original portion may be the right wing with the half-story garret windows. The left wing, a full two stories in height, may have been added in the 1860s. By 1874 H. Landin is identified as the owner in Beers' atlas. This was probably Robert Landin. Robinson's 1898 atlas shows Dawson Landin Jr. residing here.

Lois remembers "Uncle Will" Bishop and his wife Lena ("Aunt Lena") Landin Bishop living here during the 1940s. Aunt Lena was the sister of Uncle Billy Landin.

The hedge, shrubs and fruit trees seen so clearly in this view are of special interest.

187 Sharrott's Road

Photograph by Percy L. Sperr, May 12, 1937. Milstein Division of United States History, Local History & Genealogy, The New York Public Library, Astor, Lenox and Tilden Foundations. 1253 B7. No. 187, like No. 183, was built by a member of the Winant family, probably before 1850. R. Winant's name appears in this location on Butler's map of 1853. The earlier part of the house is on the left. It has three bays and half-story windows on the second floor. The two-column porch appears to be a 20th-century addition.

This became the home of oysterman Dawson Landin Sr. before 1874 (Beers' atlas, 1874). By 1907 it had become the home of Dawson Landin Jr., Lois Mosley's maternal grandfather (E. Robinson's atlas, 1907). On Sept. 12, 1923, Susan Landin and Howard Henry were married here. They became Lois's parents. Lois visited her grandmother Georgiana Landin frequently here, where they slept in the featherbed. She remembers "Uncle" Dan Green, who lived in the small wing on the right. Harriet was Green's wife's. She died before Lois was born.

187 and 183 Sharrott's Road

Photograph by Loring McMillen, Dec. 31, 1933. SIHS. The two neighboring houses stand out against the snow-covered landscape. The wide clapboard on No. 187 *(left)* is clearly visible. It had lost most of its paint by the time this photograph was made.

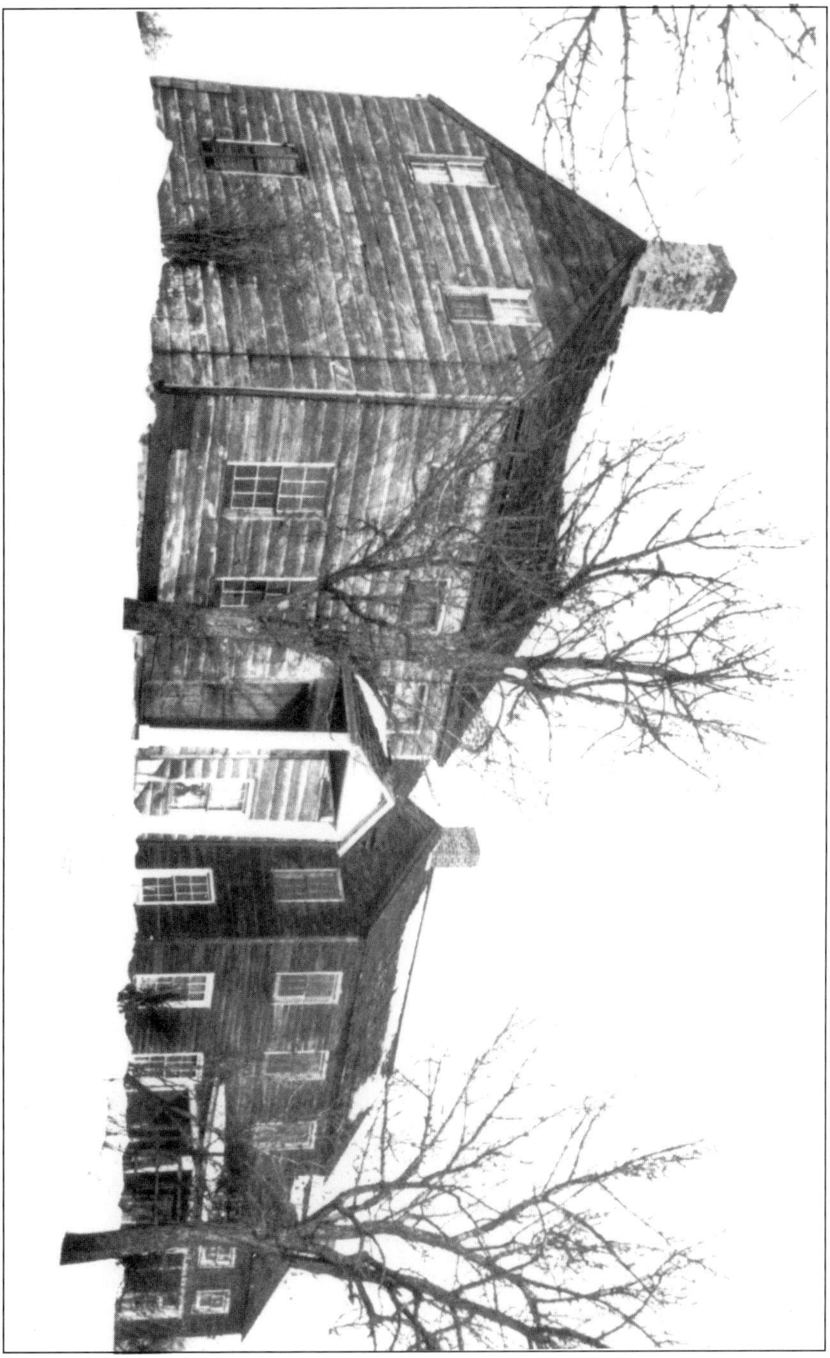

INSET: Joseph Bishop at Bishop's Forge. *New York Daily News Sunday Magazine, April 2, 1978.*

Woodrow Road

Bishop's Forge, 1448 Woodrow Road

Joseph Bishop (1906-1986) was known for making wagon wheels out of iron. He shoed horses up until 1932. He also made ornamental ironwork. The date of this building's construction, probably around 1920, has not been documented.

Joseph's father, William A. Bishop, who died ca. 1934, had built a forge across the street. His blacksmithing business began there in 1888. William forged tools used in the oyster industry, later changing to more general ironwork. Joseph learned forging from his father.

William's father, Joseph, was a woodworker who came to Sandy Ground from Snow Hill, Maryland. He died ca. 1900. (Sources: Joseph Mitchell's notes and Lois's scrapbook.)

Joseph Bishop donated Bishop's Forge to the Sandy Ground Historical Society. It was destroyed by fire in October 1982. The ruins were demolished by New York City in 1992. *(Staten Island Advance,* Feb. 19, 1998, p. A1.)

Bishop's Forge, 1448 Woodrow Road

Photograph: Anthony Lanza, ca. 1978. SIHS. The sign above the double doors reads: "Est. 1888, Joseph Bishop, Ornamental & General IRONWORK, 1448 Woodrow Rd." Wrought iron railings can be seen to the left. The 1888 date refers to his father's business.

1460 Woodrow Road

The Bishop house. This small clapboard 19th-century house has an addition with a shed roof. Three generations of the Bishop family lived here: The name of Joseph Bishop appears on this property in Sanborn's 1898 atlas. Joseph Bishop (1906-1986), his grandson, was one of five children. His mother was Laura.

1482 Woodrow Road

Several generations of one family lived here. It was the home of the Rev. Isaac Coleman, minister of the Rossville A.M.E. Zion Church, and his wife Rebecca Gray Coleman. In 1871 Stephen and Martha Gray and children came to live here with Mrs. Coleman, Stephen's mother. (The Rev. Coleman, her second husband, had died.) Rebecca Gray Landin, daughter of Stephen and Martha, lived here with her husband Robert H. Landin. She acquired several Sandy Ground properties, including the boarding houses on Bloomingdale Road. Vera Landin Usry, the Landins' daughter, lived here with her husband, William Usry. Yvonne Usry Taylor, their daughter, provided this information. This house still stands.

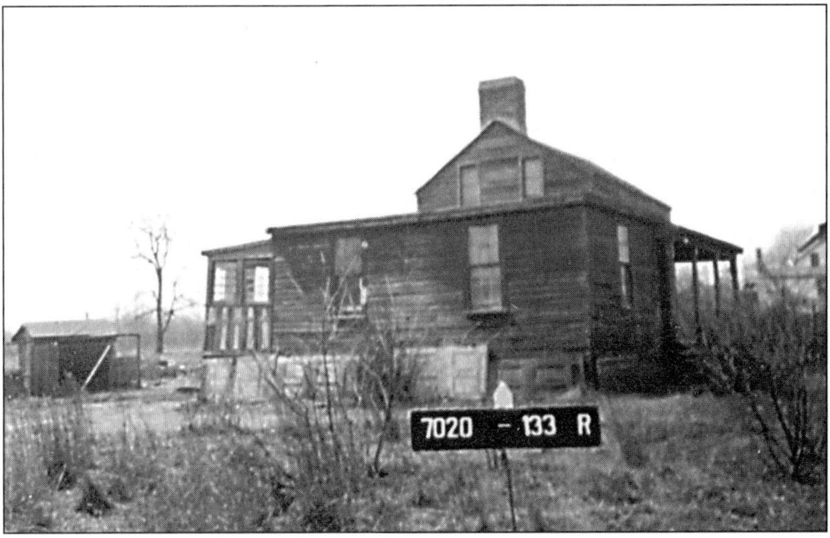
7020 - 133 R

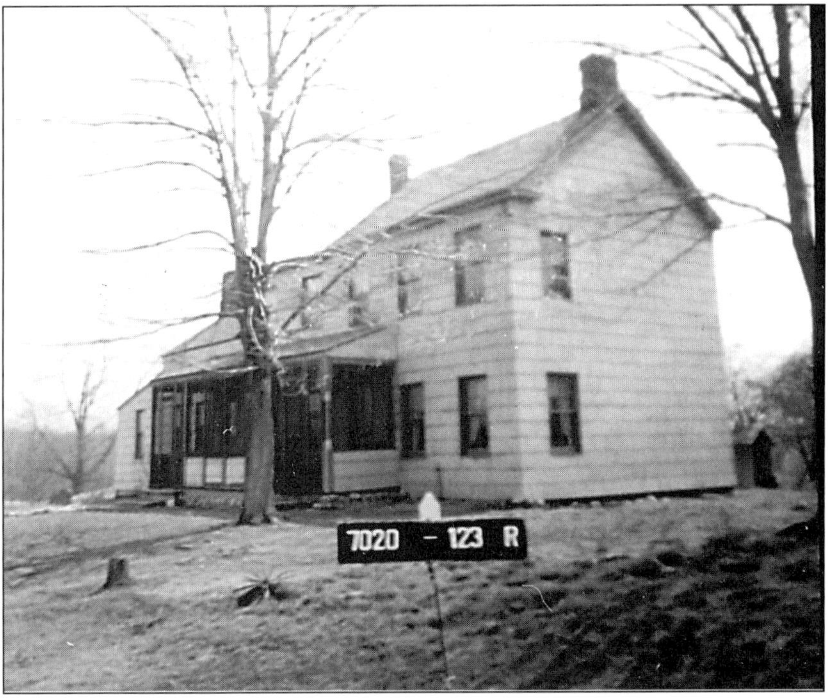
7020 - 123 R

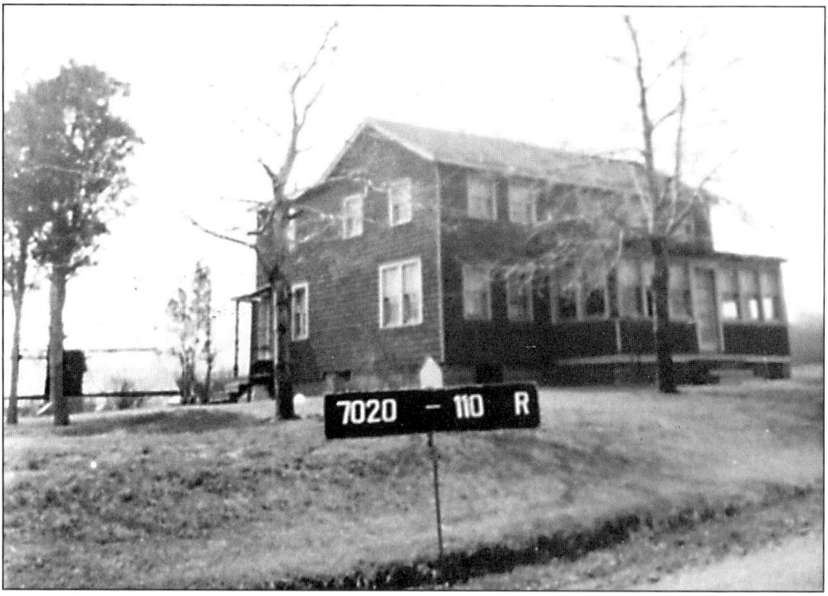
7020 - 110 R

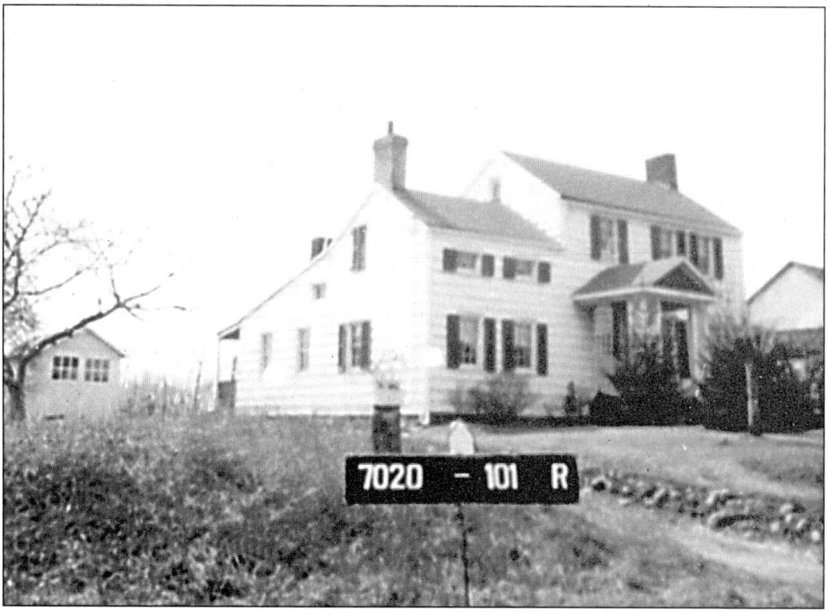
7020 - 101 R

1498 Woodrow Road

This house was owned by Abram and Arlena Decker. It is a five-bay house with shingle siding and enclosed front porch. Abram Decker was a building maintenance engineer. Mabel Decker, their daughter, married Bromley Munro in 1934. He was a successful florist. The Munros lived here with the Deckers. A large greenhouse appears in the backyard on the left.

1530 Woodrow Road

In the 1930s and 1940s the Buehl family, who were white, lived here. Yvonne Taylor, who lived at 1482 Woodrow Road, remembers Mr. Buehl in suit and tie passing her house each day on his way to work in Manhattan. This house was probably built before 1850 and is one of the oldest houses in the area. It still stands, but in a much altered state.

1538 Woodrow Road

In the 1930s this house was owned by the Bishop family, who were white. (Source: Yvonne Taylor.) Today it is the home of the Sandy Ground Historical Society.

1546 Woodrow Road

This house was probably built in the early 19th century or even the late 18th century, as suggested by its overall proportions and shallow eave. During the 1930s it was owned by the Newtons, a white family. Mr. Newton owned a taxi stand in competition with Fred Roach. A Newton daughter married Freeman Prasse of 535 Bloomingdale Road.

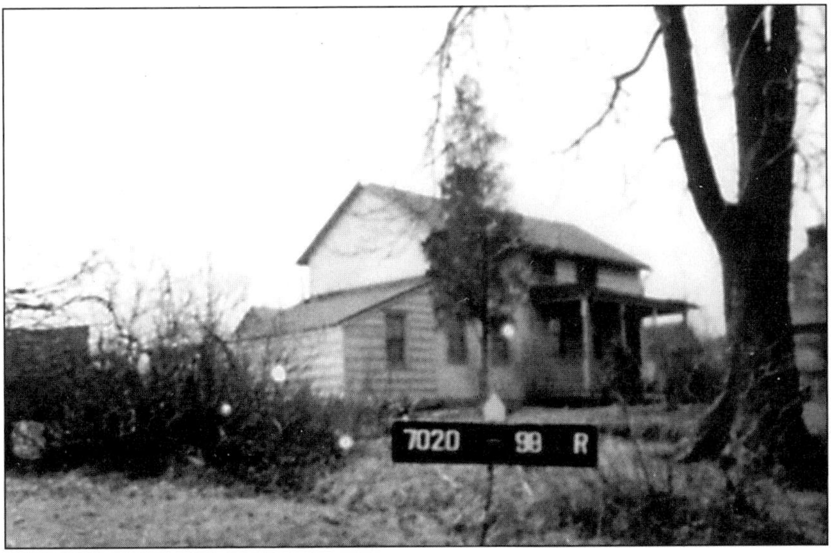
7020 - 98 R

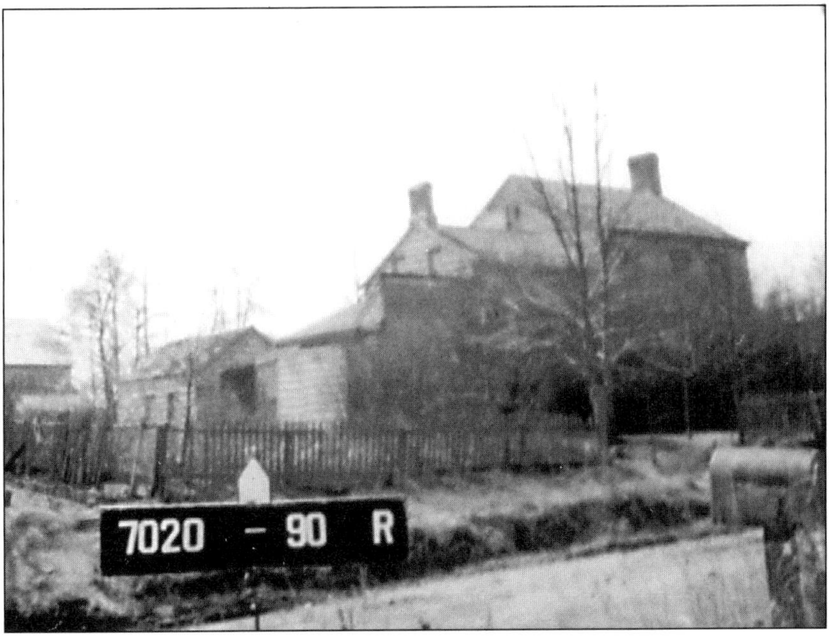
7020 - 90 R

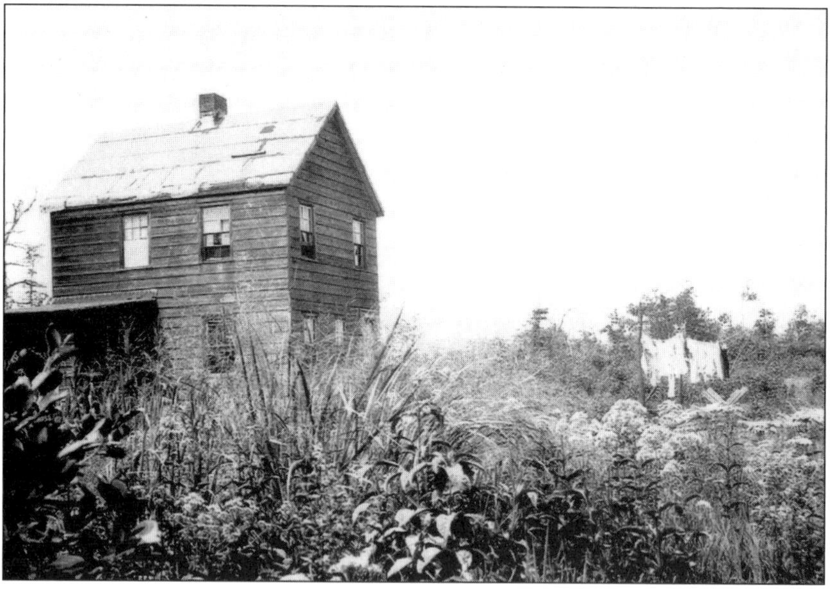

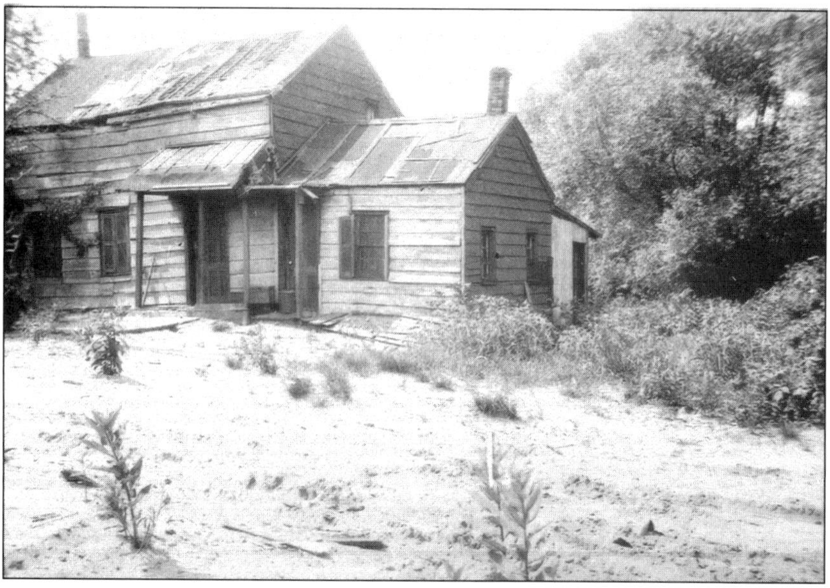

Unidentified Sandy Ground Locations

"Africa, near Pleasant Plains, Aug. 20, 1932."

Photograph by William T. Davis. SIIAS, Davis Collection No. 3620. This house appears derelict and abandoned, except for the clothes hanging out to dry. Its unpainted, wide clapboards and tar paper roofing suggest the poverty of the Great Depression. Scrub woodland in the background adds to this desolation. The lush and varied plant material in the foreground may have been Davis's primary interest in taking the photograph.

"June 23, 1933."

Photograph by William T. Davis. SIIAS. Davis Collection No. 3620.2. Sandy Ground's sandy soil is most evident in front of this perhaps abandoned house. The two front doors suggest that it may have been a two-family house.

"Bloomingdale Road, Sandy Ground."

Photographer and date unknown, SIHS.

"Sandy Ground."

Photographer and date unknown. SIHS, Accession 53. The clothing of the African American woman in her long white apron suggests a date of ca. 1900. The two front doors imply a two-family house.

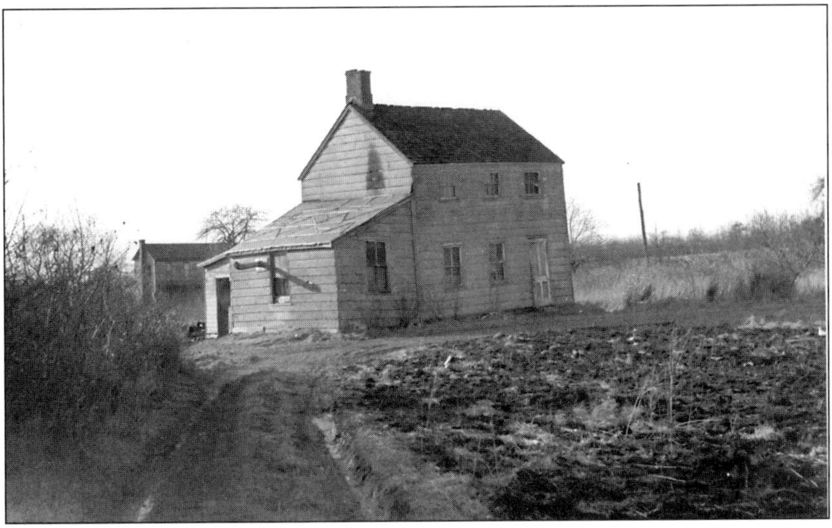

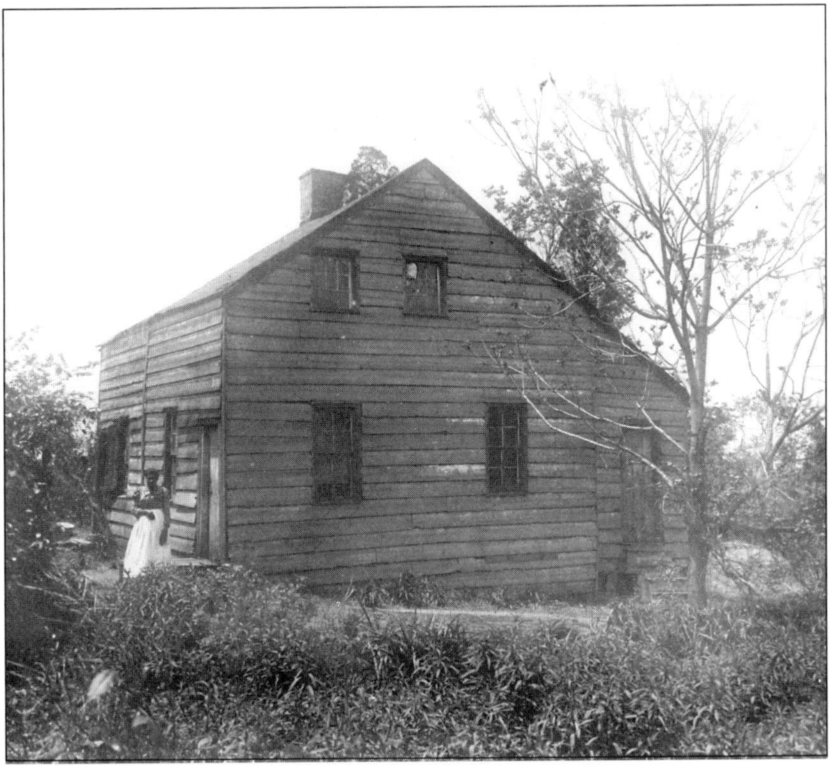

Generation Chart for
Lois Augustus Henry Mosley

Compiled by Barnett Shepherd

HOWARD CLAYTON HENRY

father's line

b. 1901 Sandy Ground, S.I.

d. 1979 Long Branch, N.J.

LOIS AUGUSTA

b. 1926   Sandy Ground, S.I.

m. Glemby Mosley

b. 1927   Bayonne, N.J.

m. 1923 Sandy Ground, S.I.

m2. Virginia Jeffers (d. 1939)

SUSAN ANN LANDIN

mother's line

b. 1905 Sandy Ground, S.I.

d. 1948 Sandy Ground, S.I.

FIFTH GENERATION   FOURTH GENERATION

JOHN JACKSON HENRY
b. 1822 Richmond Co.

FRANCES JACKSON

FRANCIS MATTHIAS HENRY
b. 1863 Richmond Co.
d. 1930 Sandy Gd, S.I.

m. 1886 Sandy Gd, S.I.
2 m. Mamie Bishop

ELIZABETH CORNELIUS
b. ca. 1825 N.Y.

ROBERT LANDIN
b. 1830 Maryland

MARY EMILY LANDIN
b. 1862 Richmond Co.
d. 1910 Sandy Gd, S.I.

SARAH JANE

DAWSON LANDIN
b. 1828 Maryland
d. 1899

DAWSON LANDIN, JR.
b. 1870

1. HARRIET
2. Mary E.

OMER HARRIS
b. ca. 1820 N.Y.

GEORGIANA HARRIS
b. 1883 Richmond Co.
d. 1936 Sandy Gd, S.I.

JOSEPHINE ROACH
b ? N.Y.C.

THIRD GENERATION   SECOND GENERATION   FIRST GENERATION

Notes for Generation Chart for
Lois Augusta Henry Mosley

I. Henry Line

First Generation

Frances Jackson was the sister of Captain John Jackson (1777?-1863). She was the mother of John Jackson Henry and Elizabeth Henry Titus. Source: Wilkins, 1989, p. 7 and Joseph Mitchell's notes, p. 5.

Second Generation

Children of John Jackson Henry (b. 1822) and Elizabeth Cornelius Henry (b. 1825?)

1. Josephine (b. 1848?)
2. Augusta (b. 1852 or 53) I believe this is the same child as Sarah Ann Augusta Henry. (Sarah A. F.(?) in census of 1855.)
3. Francis (b. 1863)

Source of Elizabeth's family name is Wilkins, 1989, p. 7. Sources of Elizabeth's name and the names of the children are the censuses of 1865 and 1870. The 1875 census indicates that his wife's name is Sarah Ann, presumably a second marriage or an error.

Third Generation

The Children of Francis Matthias Henry (1863-1930) and Mary Emily Landin (1862-1910) m.2 Mamie Bishop

1. Flora (1892-1974)
   not married
2. Fred (1893-1973)
   m. Marie Rogers
      3 sons
3. Everett (1896-1980)
   m. Edna
      2 daughters
4. Edith (d. 1-14-44)
   m. John Gibbs, lived Perth Amboy
      4 daughters
5. Lillian Augusta (d. 12-16-57)
   not married
6. Helen (1899-1986)
   not married
      1 son
7. Howard Clayton (1901-1977)
   m. Susan Landin (1905-1948)
      4 children
   m 2. Virginia Jeffers
8. Evelyn (d. 1970)
   m. Louis Pennyfeather, lived Perth Amboy
      1 daughter
9. Roy Bishop (1918-1993)
   not married

Source: Lois Mosley's Notebook

Fourth Generation

The Children of Howard Clayton
Henry (1901-1979) and Susan
Landin Henry (1905-1948)

1. Howard Kenneth ("Hash")
   (b.1924-1979)
   m. Doris Blackwell
2. Lois Augusta (b. 1926)
   m. Glemby Mosley (b. 4-18-27)
3. Mary Emily (b. 1928)
   m. Elmer Cooper
   4 daughters
4. Frances Helen (b. 1930)
   m. Woodrow Hemmingway
   3 children
   m 2. Vincent Joseph

Source: Lois Mosley

II. Robert Landin line

First Generation

No information

Second Generation

Children of Robert Landin (1830-
1910) and Sarah Jane Landin

1. Esther C. (b. ca. 1857)
2. Sarah H. (b. ca. 1859)
   m. Bishop
3. Mary Emily (b. 1862)
   m. Henry
4. Emily J.
   m. Henman
5. William A.
6. Lucy A.
   m. Alston

7. Ruth
8. Robert Jr. (b. 1865)
9. William D. (b. ca. 1867)
10. Charles

Source: Census 1875 does not use
initial H. in Robert Landin's name.
Hubble does use the initial H. and
provides name of his wife. The Census of 1875 gives the names of earlier
children. Deed Liber 374 Page 134
gives later children.

I have chosen to drop the initial H.
to avoid confusion with Robert H.
Landin (1854-1881) who resided on
Woodrow Road. The relationship be-
tween Robert Landin and Robert H.
Landin, if any, has not been determined.

III. Dawson Landin line

First Generation

No information

Second Generation

The Children of Dawson Landin
(1828-1899) and his wife
   1 m. Harriet
   2 m. Mary E.
1. Mary Elizabeth (b. Nov. 28, 1850)
   m. Jones
2. William H. (b. June 15, 1853)
3. Susan A. (b. Mar. 10, 1855)
   m. Walker
   no children
4. Harriett (b. Jul. 8, 1857)
   m. Green

5. William James (b. Apr. 5, 1859)
6. Emily Moriah (b. Jan. 18, 1860)
7. Sarah Frances (b. May 17, 1863
    m. Jackson
    daughter: Harriett
    m. Stotswood
    daughter: Cecelia E. (b. Oct. 20, 1887)
    m. Smith
8. Ellen Luser (b. Apr. 12, 1867)
9. Dawson Landin Jr. (b. Apr. 9, 1870)
    m. Georgianna Harris (1883-1936)
    children: see below

Source: Harriet Landin's name as wife of Dawson Landin is found in the Richmond County census of 1875, transcribed by Richard Dickenson. The name of Dawson Landin's second wife, Mary E., is provided by Deeds of Richmond County Liber 410 Page 376.

Family Bible page with above list of children and birth dates was found in a dumpster at 26 Clay Pit Road and is now (2002) in the collection of Lois Mosley.

Deeds of Richmond County Libers 410 page 587 and Liber 410 page 374 give married names of several of these children after death of Dawson Landin, Sr.

Third Generation
The Children of Dawson H. Landin (b. 1870) and Georgianna Harris (1883-1936).

1. Gertrude (b. 1898)
   not married
2. Frances (b. 1901)
   m. Murphy Moore from Virginia
   1. Lenora
   2. Lindwood
   3. Beatrice
   4. Calvin (drowned)
3. Susan (1904-1948)
   m. Howard Clayton Henry (1901-1979)
   5 children
4. Kenneth (b. 1917)
   m. Anna Mae Tullah
   5 boys

Source: Lois Mosley Notebook

IV. Omer Harris line

First Generation
No information

Second Generation
Children of Omer Harris (b. 1820?) and Josephine Roach
1. Augustine (f)
   m. James
2. Charles
   m. Ethel Mangin
3. Ella
   m. Moody
4. Georgiana (1883—1936)
   m. Dawson Landin, Jr.
5. Edna
   not married

A Note Concerning Moses K. Harris and Silas K. Harris

I have not been able to establish the kinship, if any, between Omer Harris (Lois Mosley's maternal great-grandfather) and the brothers Moses K. Harris and Silas K. Harris, who are among the earliest documented founders of Sandy Ground. However, they were all of the same generation, and may have been relatives.

Children of Moses K. Harris and Louisa Harris

1. Richard (b. ca. 1845)
2. Ida (b. ca. 1847)
3. William (b. ca. 1847)
4. Moses (b. ca. 1849)
   m. 1875 Sarah Ann Augusta Henry
5. Louisa (b. ca. 1854)
6. Omer (b. 1856)
7. Andrew

Source: The names of Moses's wife and children are listed in the New York State Census of 1855 and the Federal Census of 1860.

The marriage of Moses (the son) to Sarah Ann Augusta Henry in 1875 is found in Vosburgh's transcription (p. 95) of the Records of the Woodrow Methodist Episcopal Church. This is the only reference in Vosburgh's transcription to African Americans.